I0480091

EVERY-DAY ART.

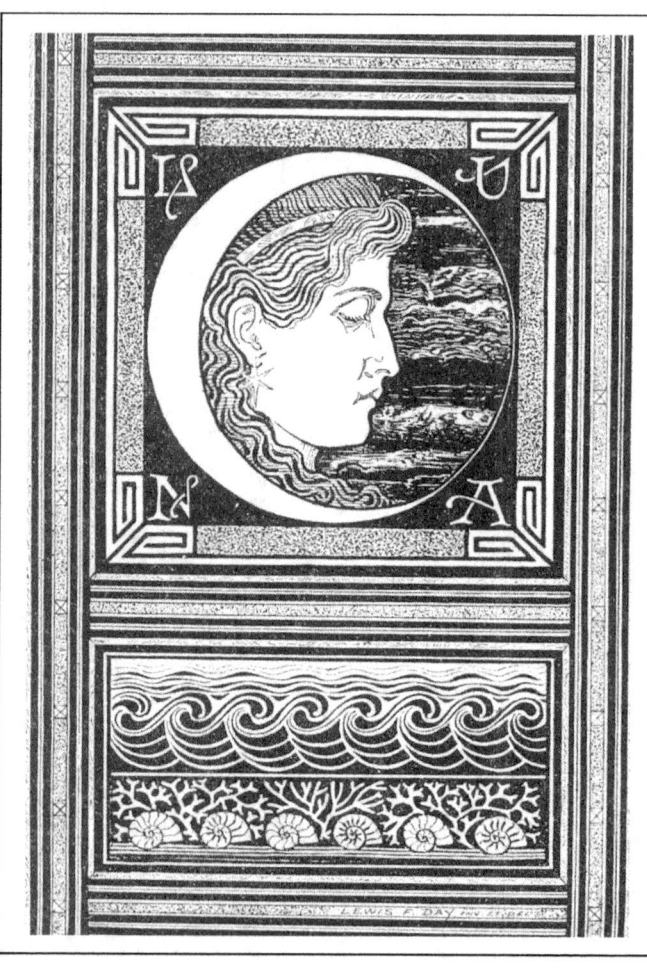

EVERY-DAY ART:

SHORT ESSAYS ON THE ARTS NOT FINE,

BY

LEWIS FOREMAN DAY,

AUTHOR OF 'INSTANCES OF ACCESSORY ART,' &c.

" *De gustibus* EST *disputandum*."

NUMEROUS ILLUSTRATIONS, CHIEFLY BY THE AUTHOR.

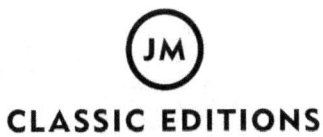

CLASSIC EDITIONS

This edition digitally re-mastered and
published by JM Classic Editions © 2008
Original text © Lewis F Day 1882

ISBN 978-1-906600-07-5

All rights reserved. No part of this book subject
to copyright may be reproduced in any form or
by any means without prior permission in writing
from the publisher.

TO THE READER.

WRITINGS on art divide themselves mainly into two kinds—the technical and the readable.

Of these the one class appeals necessarily to a limited public, and is seldom calculated to tempt a reader not deeply concerned in the subject. The other has a value chiefly literary, and scarcely appeals to the student of art.

It has been my endeavour to keep a middle course, and to find readable expression for matter which is of a more or less technical character. I have tried to present my thoughts in a form as perfect as is within the reach of one whose every-day art is not of a literary nature; but though I have not relied upon the reader's interest in ornament, my words are addressed, in the first place, to those who know, or wish to know, something of it.

Some there may be to whom these essays will not be the less interesting from the fact, that they originated in my having something to say about my art, instead of having to say something.

LEWIS F. DAY.

13, *Mecklenburg Square, London*, 1882.

NOTE.

It was impossible for me to express myself on the subject of Every-day Art, without repeating something of what I had already said in the pages of the 'Magazine of Art' and elsewhere. Whenever that has been necessary, and it has seemed to me that I could not better the words I had already used, I have allowed them to stand. But nothing has been included here without reconsideration, and revision; and in many cases I have entirely recast the original thought. By arrangement with Messrs. Cassell, Petter & Galpin, the publisher of this volume is enabled to add considerably to the number of illustrations, without proportionately increasing the price of the book.

L. F. D.

CONTENTS.

Part I.

Contents.

Part II.

LIST OF ILLUSTRATIONS.

PART I.

ERRATA.

Page   6. — Top line, for " omnipotent," read " omnipresent."

   ,,   110.—Thirteenth line from bottom of page, for " material forms," read " natural forms."

EVERY-DAY ART.

PART I.

ON ORNAMENT.

"Orno, Ornas, Ornat, Ornamus, Ornatis, Ornant."

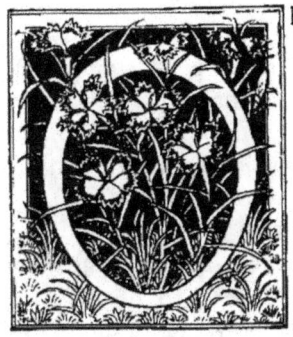 RNAMENT is the art of every-day. The great picture galleries may be likened to the temples of art, whither devout worshippers, and others less devout but no less anxious to pass for pious, resort only at intervals. So, also, a treasured painting may be the shrine at which a man offers up in private the incense of his admiration. But every day and all day long we breathe the atmosphere of ornament. There is no escape from its influence. Good or bad, it pervades every object with which our daily doings bring us in contact. We may, if we choose, keep away from picture galleries

and not look at pictures ; but, our attention once turned to ornament, we can no longer shut our eyes and decline to take heed of it, though there are all about us forms of it which every cultivated man would evade at any cost if he could. It may be to us a dream of beauty or a horrible nightmare, but we cannot shake it off. At every turn in life we come face to face with some fresh phase of it.

The question of ornament is, therefore, neither insignificant nor one that has significance only for the wealthy few. Neither is it a matter which concerns only those who take some interest in art, since we are all of us, however little inclined towards the arts, alike compelled to ornament our dwellings, our belongings, and ourselves.

Imagine for a moment how a man would set about furnishing a house without art. In the first place the house itself would need to be built for him, and not a door, or window-frame, or chimney-piece, not so much as a fire-grate, door-knocker, or area-railing, but would have to be made to his express order. The furniture, from the door-scraper to his easy chair, would in like manner have to be designed for him ; and it is doubtful whether the markets of the known world would suffice to supply the necessary utensils, implements, and household vessels, all innocent of ornament. Were this at last accomplished, the first time he entered it he himself would introduce within its walls the inevitable decoration—unless, indeed, he put off on the door-step the clothes that the usages of society have deter- mined to be neces- sary ap- pendages to the natural man. The cut of his coat, or the rib of the cloth, the polish of his boots, the curve of his hat-brim, the shape of his studs, the pat- tern of his watch-chain, the starch of his linen, the knot of his necktie, the ring on his finger, the umbrella in his hand, even the all-necessary money in his pocket, would any one of them be enough to destroy the artless simplicity at which he vainly aimed. A lady enter- ing in every-day walking cos- tume would introduce a small museum of ornamental detail.

You cannot so much as ac- cept the present of a box of

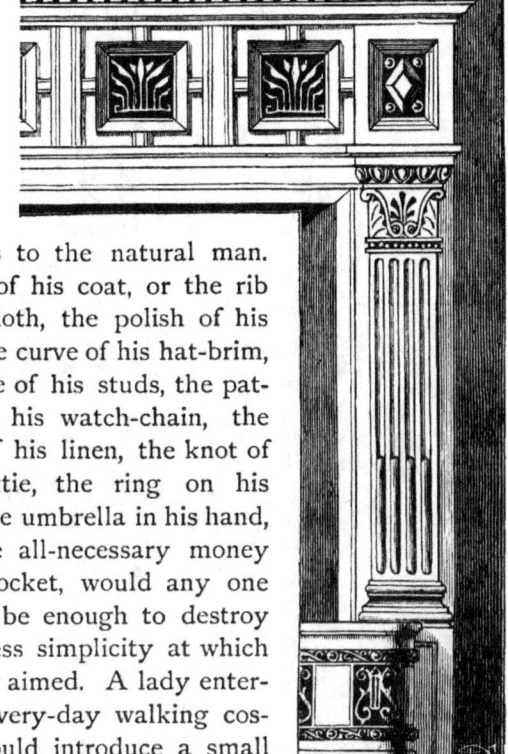

Instances of ornament.

Elvas plums without at the same time receiving food for thought on ornament. There is the pattern of red and green printed on the paper with which it is covered, bearing distinctly the date of its design upon it, and illustrating the very simplest form of

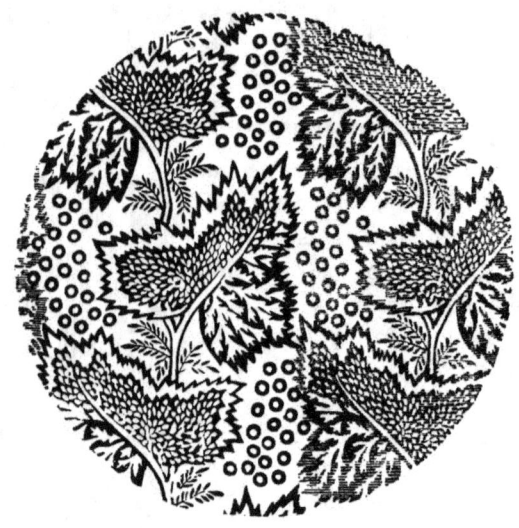

Box-top.

printing. Something might be said also as to the relation of its stripes to the circular shape of the box. Then we find inside a disc of cut paper, delightfully naïve in its perforation, and exemplifying to perfection the adaptation of design to the method of its execution. No less suggestive of the scissors are the shreds of tinsel mingled with the plums ; and the barbaric richness of their effect in the box is admirable. But there is a warning in them, too. They have a way of adhering to the fruit ; and you

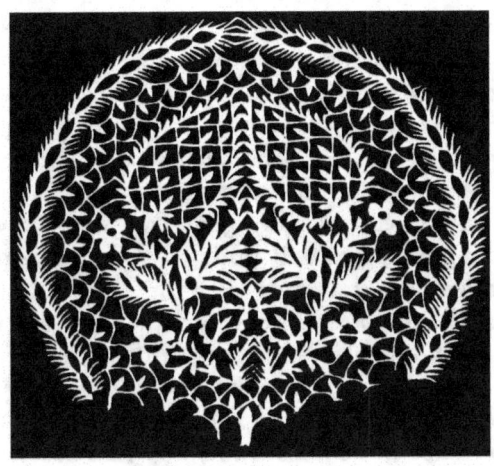

Cut-paper ornament.

relish the tinsel less when it gets between your teeth.

The love of decoration is not a characteristic peculiar to this year of grace. Ornament dates back to the rudimentary stage of the human race. If we were to trace it to its beginnings, we should find ourselves in Eden—or in monkeydom. To-day it is omnipotent among us ; and we can scarcely conceive a "coming race" without ornament.

The association of art with every common object of daily use seems to be in the natural order of things. It was so in Ancient Greece and Rome, and during the Renaissance. The ruder Gothic craftsmen and the earlier Egyptians and Assyrians were no exceptions to the rule. So also the Arab artists, all over the Eastern world, delighted to find in every branch of handiwork excuse for the elaboration of ingenious ornament. Even among the aborigines of Mexico, New Zealand, and the South Sea Islands, we find that every opportunity for ornament was seized, necessity guiding it into the way it should go. It was only during a period of almost utter dearth of art among us, in the eighteenth and first half of the present centuries, that the idea was entertained that use and ornament were in any sense antagonistic. The result of attempting to draw the line between use and ornament, as if the two were not to be reconciled, was that ornament, which is irrepressible, struck out on its own account, and, unrestrained by sober use, indulged in all the extravagance and excess which the better taste of the last few years has "scotched" but scarcely killed.

Perhaps we may assume, since there is usually some ground in fact for every fiction, that it was the perversion of ornamental art among civilised nations, subsequent to the degradation of Renaissance design, which led to the idea that use and ornament were incompatible. Let us hope that the recurrence to a better style of decorative design among us in this generation, and a truer appreciation of the end and object of ornament, will finally overturn this fallacy; so that not even the most practical and prosaic person shall be able to rest in the belief that use and ornament are independent one of the other. For decoration is, or should be, art controlled by common sense.

It is beyond dispute that the influence of our every-day surroundings must affect us, and possibly they influence us much more powerfully than we are accustomed to suspect. That some among us should be doomed to live without beauty is deeply to be deplored ; such poor creatures may find relief in deadening the sense of beauty within them, but it can never be quite the same thing to us whether we live in the midst of beauty or of ugliness.

Æsthetic culture is not the high-road to all the virtues, and, indeed, certain of the vices have been known to infest it. Neither, on the other hand, is there any special grace in ugliness. Art is only utterance. It must express something ; and the vital question is, what does it express ? The daily association with honest, manly, real work, with graceful fancy, individual character, and refined art, must exert on us an influence less demoralising than the continual contact with falsity, pretence, and affectation. The fact that we may be wholly unconscious of the influence about us does not destroy its effect. The fresh air is tonic, whether we feel it to be so or not ; and the germs of disease that emanate from a foul atmosphere are none the less fatal, though our nostrils be not sufficiently delicate to make us aware of the poison we breathe.

The low condition to which ornament had fallen until within the last twenty or thirty years, accounts fully for the slight esteem in which it has come to be held ; and there is little doubt that improved design will in time restore to decoration the prestige that attached to it as a matter of course in days when art and handicraft were scarcely distinguishable, and easel pictures were not accounted the be-all and end-all of art. Those were days when artists of eminence did not disdain to do work which is now left to mechanics, and even owed sometimes their distinction to success in it. Already there is a current of reaction in this respect, and perhaps even a danger that the cause of decorative art may be swamped in a wave of fashion, to be left presently high and dry beyond the reach of public sympathy. However that may be, popular interest in the industrial or rather the decorative arts appears to be growing ; and there is some ground for hope that the change may be lasting, inasmuch as this interest is no new thing, but a recurrence to that catholic appreciation of the arts which has characterised all periods when art has thriven. To-day's interest in decorative art may be only a fashion. It is more encouraging to believe that yesterday's apathy was but an episode.

TASTE.

"I know what I like!"

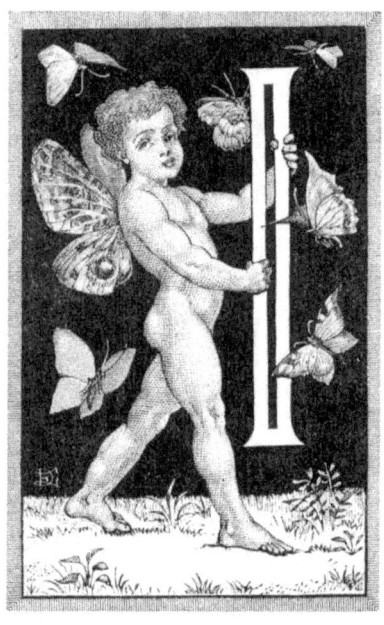

T is characteristic of decorative art that it depends almost as much upon the critical as upon the creative faculty of the artist. More than any other art it depends upon taste; and by that test it stands or falls. It is taste that determines— what is it that it does not determine in decoration ? It settles in the first place whether there shall be decoration at all, of what kind it shall be, and how executed, where introduced, and to what extent.

It prescribes what is wanted, what is admissible, and what is becoming. Not one of these questions can be solved without reference to it. Every work of applied art is a problem, and the most important factor in its solution is taste.

This, too, is worthy to be remembered, that whilst we judge of a man's power by the height of his highest achievement, we measure his taste less generously, not even according to the average of his work, but by his weakest. When once an artist has succeeded in producing a powerful impression, it survives many failures. We point to his great work and say : That shows what he could do ! But a single false step in taste is fatal ; it is difficult to believe any more in the certainty of a judgment that has once been flagrantly at fault ; we think always of the man's failure, and wonder : How can he ever have let that pass ?

There is unconscious recognition of the supremacy of the faculty in the tacit assumption that every educated man or woman is *de facto* already gifted with taste. So firmly is this infatuation rooted in men's minds that it amounts to an insult to question their authority in this respect. Is not every alderman a man of taste? We have all of us met ere now the worthy gentleman who "knows what he likes," and who announces that incontrovertible fact with a self-satisfaction which seems to imply that really it is no slight merit in him that he knows no more. It would be, of course, the height of rudeness to suggest in answer, that his preference did not of necessity argue excellence. But why is it that in this matter of art a man, even while admitting that he knows nothing of the subject, will protest that he is none the less competent to give judgment? He would hesitate with regard to any other subject to pit his ignorance against the special knowledge of an expert.

The confusion in men's minds is owing in part to a confusion of the different senses in which the word is used. Bad taste may mean bad breeding, and no one cares to be accused of that. Again, taste may be understood to signify liking, and in respect to liking every man must be a law to himself. There is no disputing on that point. Even though it be raw spirit that we prefer to mellow wine, or crude combinations of red, blue, and yellow that we like better than any subtle harmony of colour, we have a perfect right to our preference. Whether by announcing it we show discrimination or expose our ignorance, concerns no one but ourselves.

In reference to art there should be no mistake about the meaning of the word. Liking is one thing, and taste quite another. One may heartily dislike a work of art, and yet acknowledge that it is good ; and the faculty that enables us to realise that fact is taste. A competent critic, if he be honest, admits in calmer moments that his judgment is biassed by personal predilection, and that he is not unerring. It is reserved for the average English gentleman to assume calmly that his likes and dislikes constitute good and bad in art—only in art. In other respects he is sane enough. He does not argue with his solicitor or pretend to prescribe to his physician. He goes to them for advice, and whether he acts upon it or not, the fact that he is prepared to pay for it argues that he attaches some value to it. It is true that society does not insist that a man should be versed in the law or in medicine, and that it does demand that he should be able to converse about art. Society, by the way, appears to be quite innocent of what nonsense he talks when he begins. If for a moment he could but see himself as artists see him !

The expression of a man's honest preference, without prejudice and without affectation, is valuable in proportion to his experience and character ; and there is no particular reason why he should keep it to himself ; but the cool way in which those who never held a brush since the days of their childhood pretend to determine what is good and bad, "well painted," or "out of drawing," would be amusing, if it did not stand in the way of all true appreciation of what they are talking about. Lookers-on see the best of the game, it is true, but not unless they know its rules. For every fault that the mere *dilettante* really discovers in a work of art, there are possibly a dozen merits that he fails to detect ; and

if he flatters himself that he has detected precious
qualities in a work unrecognised by the profession,
the probable reason for its neglect (if it have indeed
the merit he sees) is that it is marred by grave
faults of execution of which he has no suspicion.
It would be only decently modest in him to assume
that, whenever he differs from an artist as to a
matter of art which he has himself not particularly
studied, he is in the wrong ; for the artist probably
has studied it. Directly we go beyond the expression of personal opinion, and venture to say
what is good or bad, we assume the function of
critic, an assumption which can only be justified by
the knowledge and experience that come of diligent
and earnest study.

There is no more common pretence than that of
a knowledge of art ; and though the affectation is
evident at once to those who really know, it is
difficult to prove to those whom it has duped, how
hollow it is. The best in art can only be demons-
trated by appealing to faculties that comparatively
few persons possess, and that still fewer have
cultivated. Ignorance mostly pays a penalty of
some sort, and the payment buys knowledge. The
man whose palate is not so delicate but that he
enjoyed the wine he drank last night, may be convinced, if only by the logic of this morning's headache, that it was not of the best, and begin
to mistrust his judgment accordingly ; but the
indulgence in ignorance of art pays no such

obvious toll—there is no headache afterwards.
It seems almost ungracious to attempt to persuade
a man that he has purchased a vile work of art ;
and his vanity, and the want of discernment that
permitted the purchase, together, make his en-
lightenment all but impossible   The thing remains
before his eyes, henceforth further to vitiate his
sense of what is beautiful.   "After all," says the
popular fallacy, "it is a matter of taste !"   But
taste is not a personal matter.   It is no more
mere preference than judgment is mere opinion.
It is as rare as it is supposed to be common.   It
implies not only artistic feeling and critical power,
but their cultivation too.   Failing artistic sympathy,
we miss the very aroma of the art we profess to
judge ; without critical faculty we are inevitably
led away by our feelings ; and without experience
we are in danger of mistaking molehills for moun-
tains, never having seen such a thing as a mountain.

In all his work the artist shows something of
himself.   We see the man behind the artist : he
betrays himself by his silence as well as by his
utterance, by what he leaves undone as well as
what he does.   But if this be true of the artist's
personality, it is still more true with regard to his
culture ; and it is the evidence in a man's work of
natural artistic tact, *plus* cultivation and experience,
that we distinguish as taste.

It might well be supposed that taste, being only
the controlling and not the creative or manipulative

faculty, might be a common attribute of the more
refined and cultivated class of amateurs ; and it is
so far true that a man of culture and an amateur
is far more likely to err on the side of timidity and
safety than on that of powerful but vulgar effect.
But the fact remains that the mere looker-on does
not educate himself in anything like the degree
that the worker does. You may look at a thing
fifty times, and carefully too ; yet when you come
to copy it you find that you had not seen half that
was there. With rare exceptions, a man who has
not been himself a practical workman, does not
really know much about art workmanship ; he errs
through ignorance ; probably he adopts at second
hand the theories of another who has at least knowledge enough to impose his dicta upon him ; his
experience is limited, his eye untrained, and his
judgment mere impulse or fancy. How astonish-
ingly crude is the criticism of persons who are,
except in art, cultivated ! They do not even know
what an artist means when he talks of vulgarity in
his craft. Coarse language and loud tones, mincing
affectation and pretence, offend them ; but they
would be startled to be told that the brutal workmanship, the crude colours, the mechanical affectation of finish, and the pretentiousness of cheap
show, which are to be found broadcast in their
drawing-rooms, are simply vulgar. The cultivated
amateur has a general idea that anything very
powerful in effect approaches vulgarity. He will

scarcely dare to like it till it has received the stamp of critical approval. He judges a picture mainly according to its subject. The painting of a fish-monger's shop or an old woman peeling potatoes, may well be vulgar, he thinks ; but how can there be any vulgarity in the representation of neatly combed cows and other very clean cattle? or in devotional subjects that are conventionally correct, smooth, shiny, and altogether pretty? He thinks always more of the story than of its treatment. His criticism is as that of one who should praise an author for his taste in never using a *word* "that may offend," when the whole tenor of his writing, his very style itself, is pervaded by an undisguisable taint of commonness.

The amateur can know little of the self-restraint of the craftsman, which, to a fellow-craftsmen, is so obvious in his work ; and it is this self-restraint, this holding always a strict balance between facility and fitness, that constitutes the crowning difficulty of ornamental design. Power is proverbially impatient of restraint, and taste, in its turn, is always half afraid of force ; * yet it is on the reconciliation of this impatience with this fear that admirable decoration must depend. Some ornament is too feeble to provoke hostility ; none is so powerful as to be independent of taste.

* " Warum will sich Geschmack und Genie so selten vereinen ? Jener fürchtet die Kraft ; dieses verachtet den Zaum."
                                                                                                        Goethe.

Nor can we confidently depend either on the
teaching of nature or of ancient ornament to direct
us, for it is taste that first enables us to turn their
teaching to account. What is admirable in nature
is not always equally to be admired in art, and
the affectation of what was once true in taste ceases
to be tasteful. The modern attempts to reproduce
what was beautiful in old work are for the most
part coarse or meaningless, or both at once. Compare the tenderness of one of Lippi's angel heads
with the insipidity of the saints of recent manufacture ; or the earnestness of Early Gothic
sculpture with the heartlessness of our parodies of
it. No matter how grotesque the carving of old
gurgoyles and stall-seats, we delight in the quaintness, though there be nothing else to admire in
them ; we are not easily shocked by the inconsistencies of the simple mason, who believed in
something very like the imps that he introduced
into his work, and who scarcely

> " Knew but that the God who doth create
> And animate the whole, ...
> . . . . . . might appear
> In manifestive brightness, and array
> His being in the form the holy artist framed."

At any rate, we imagine some such feeling in
the Gothic mason, and the sentimental interest that
clings to the old work renders it sacred to us ; but
the nineteenth century affectation of ancient art is

doubly hateful to us, that we look back tenderly on the past, that we look hopefully forward to the future. Such affectation would not be tolerated for a moment in literature. We are content to enjoy the curiously homely and prosaic imagery of the religious poetry of the seventeenth century without travestying it. Fancy a modern imitation of George Herbert!

It is curious to observe how little correspondence there is between the progress of civilisation and of taste. Each appears to have gone its own way quite independently of the other.

Much of the reticence of old-world ornament is due to a kind of intuitive taste, which reveals, however, rather the simplicity of the workman, and the rudimentary nature of his appliances, than any self-restraint in him. His sense of fitness is undisturbed by any idea of even the possibility of imitating natural effects. He is quite unconscious of the excellence of his ornament. He prefers, when he once sees it, the most tawdry of European importations to anything that is produced by his tribe. His sense of what is beautiful, moreover, stops abruptly short at what is absolutely subordinate to use. The battle-clubs and paddles of savages, their basketwork and mats, are admirable ; but their idols are, without exception, monstrously ugly, and their ideal of personal adornment is apt to culminate in the distortion and mutilation of their natural bodies.

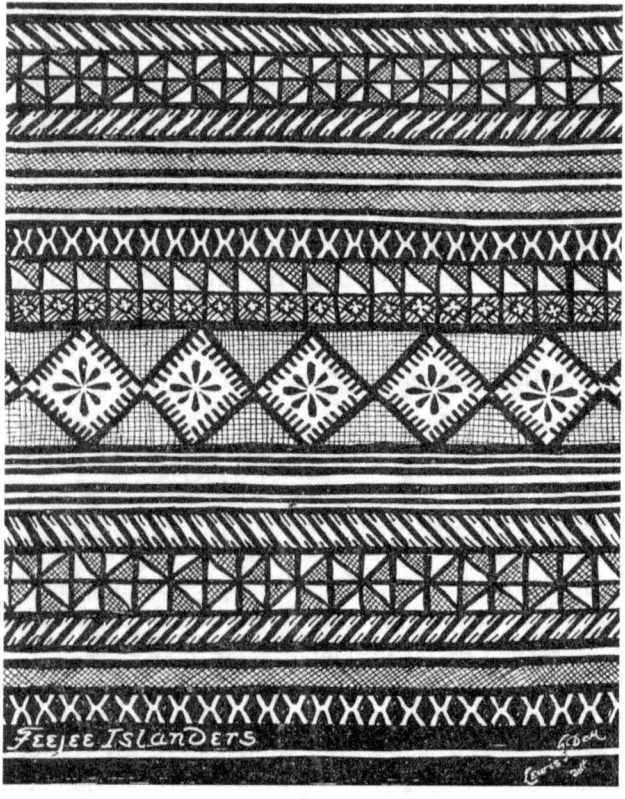

Instance of savage taste in ornament.

The more cultivated art of the Mohammedan nations is proportionately more refined and beautiful. In this ornament the self-restraint is only in obedience to the laws of the Prophet. It was religion that served as the bridle to Asiatic extravagance, and made Moresque art almost too evenly excellent.

In the art of the ancient Greeks, the most exquisite taste of all is shown ; and in their case it must be ascribed mainly to the degree of culture to which they had attained.

It would seem that the quality of taste, as revealed in the art of the past, may be the outcome either of simplicity, of submission, or of culture. Seeing that the times on which we have fallen are out of tune with simplicity, and since the sceptic spirit of the age has determined that obedience in us shall not be blind, it would seem as if modern taste must be rooted in culture.

PAST AND PRESENT.

"New lamps for old!"

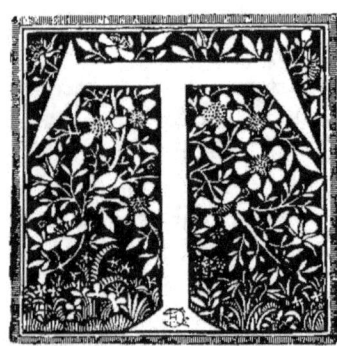

HE estimation in which men hold the work of the past ages, progresses in a somewhat curious order. In our first ignorance we condemn it as barbarous or old-fashioned ; on a slight acquaintance we begin to be attracted to it ; and by degrees we are taken captive by the charms of antiquity, and fall into a blind pedantry that can see no beauty in anything that is new. To recover from this stage of love-sickness argues a degree of native energy and independence which not all of us appear to possess.

How strangely different are the lessons that men draw from the past ! How differently they are affected by it ! One man loses his hold on principle, and is carried away in the passing current of fashion. Another is mastered by some one style, dead to the world in general, but alive to him, alluring and fascinating him until it has taken entire possession of him, and he is no more himself but the exponent of a style that has gone by. One artist finds in the very idea of style a hindrance ; it stands in his way, and he cannot get over it. Another masters a style and bends it to his own will, compelling it to conform to his individuality and express his thought. Yet another makes use of it only as foothold for some fresh venture in art.

Something is to be said for the devotee who kneels before the past and worships. But retrospect is not art ; and it is more in the spirit of the nineteenth century to accept a given style as a starting point,—not as an end. Those who went before have doubtless left tracks which must be useful to us, and we should be wasting time, were we to insist on finding out a way for ourselves where they have trodden for us a sure path ; but we need not therefore follow them into regions which we have no want nor desire to explore ; nor need we confine ourselves entirely to the beaten way. It is well to have always a pretty clear idea as to the direction in which the high road lies ; we can wander, then, widely from it without losing our bearings ; but if we are in search of something that is not quite common-place, it will serve us perhaps more often as something to depart from than as something to follow. Old work should be no more than a starting-point for the art of any but a student. In a certain sense we are all of us students, and always; but we need not, for all that, suppress what little of originality there may be in us.

The antiquarian interest in what is old, may easily overgrow in the mind the appreciation of what is beautiful.

One may know a good piece of smith's work when it occurs, without having traced the progress of the art from Tubal Cain to Bruce Talbert; one may appreciate the glory of colour in stained glass, without being familiar with all that has been done from the twelfth century to the time of Burne Jones; and, in truth—we may whisper it lowly—the men who most truly appreciate are not the antiquaries, pedants, and compilers of catalogues, but the actual artists whom it encourages and inspires, the possible artists whom it delights and satisfies. Imagine the dead looking down in spirit on their work—would any one of them feel profoundly grateful to the critic who had assigned to

Modern outcome of Etruscan ornament.

him, with whatever accuracy, his exact position in the rank of art? Yet, if that spirit had any of the artist left in him, every thrill of genuine pleasure that his work gave to an onlooker would vibrate in him again. Still, it is always those who know best who best appreciate; and in proportion to their knowledge would their appreciation be grateful to the artist's spirit.

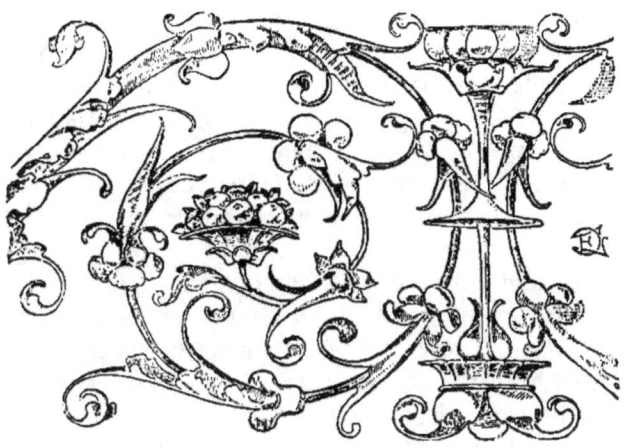

Style or fashion of François 1er.

The historic "styles" of ornament might perhaps be called only so many fashions of the past; but, at all events, they were not merely of a day or of a "season." The fashion of a century ceases to be a fashion—or, if a fashion, is no longer contemptible.

The ancient styles were not pushed and puffed into ephemeral existence; they had time to grow, develop, culminate, and at last die a natural death, the new style developing itself as naturally from their remains as a fresh plant from the seed of last autumn.

Each phase of ancient ornament embodied in some degree the ideas of the people among whom it arose, although the ideas were often, like the forms of ornament, by no means original, and the people themselves had no consciousness of any particular idea at all in the art about them. From the evidence of pots and pans alone, it would be quite safe to declare a remote people simple or sophisticated, unrefined or cultivated, sensuous or ascetic, or whatever their character might have been. In every case their ornament would betray them, and all the more surely that they did not for a moment suspect that, in the manufacture of ordinary objects of every-day use, they were writing their own history for posterity. The testimony of decorative art is, again, the more valuable in that it represents, not a single class of wealthy and perhaps cultivated purchasers of pictures, sculptures, and objects of luxury, but the whole people. Everybody had need of pots and pans, and all the multitude of common things which it came so natural to decorate that the artist was scarcely aware he had left his mark upon them.

Whatever we may think of the various styles of

ornament that have come down to us, it is impossible for us to ignore them altogether. They
are the various languages in which the past has
expressed itself, and unless we fancy in our foolish-
ness that we can evolve from inner consciousness
something at once independent of and superior to
all that has been done before our time, we must
begin by some study of the ancient principles and
practice. It will save time in the end. Even those
who flatter themselves that it will be easy for them
to take one bound into successful originality, would
do well to reflect that they are more likely to
succeed by stepping back a pace or two for a spring
than by "toeing the line."

If there were no other reason why we should
know something of past styles, it would be sufficient
that, in the absence of any marked national style
among us at present, we have taken to "reviving"
in succession all manner of bygone styles. The
ornament of to-day is to so great an extent a
reflection, in some instances a distortion, of old
work, that one cannot well discuss it without
reference to its origin. These "revivals," irrational
as they are in themselves, are not without good
results. We have such a wealth of old work about
us, accessible through modern facilities of travel,
purchasable through modern processes of reproduction, brought to our notice by modern methods of
publication, that we cannot escape their influence if
we would ; and the "revivals" have involved such a

thorough study of the various styles that, when we shall have arrived at reason and begin to express ourselves naturally in the language of our own day, it will surely tell in our work to some purpose.

It is only by the widest stretch of courtesy that the greater part of modern ornament can be called design at all. There is very little but what is borrowed. Some few of the more prominent decorative artists of our time have, indeed, established

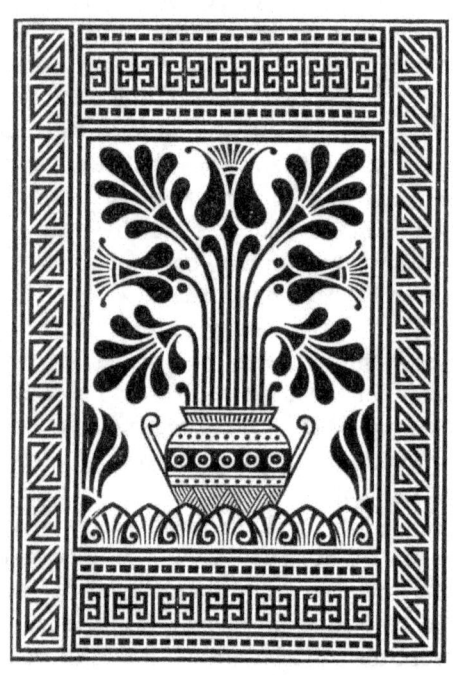

Modern ornament which is not modern.

what is to be recognised as a style of their own ; but their respective manners are probably as much the result of the study of Mediæval, Japanese,

Moresque, or Renaissance art as of their own personality. It seems as if our only opportunities for the exercise of individuality were, first, in the selection of a model, and, next, in the use we made of it. The design on ·the preceding page shows

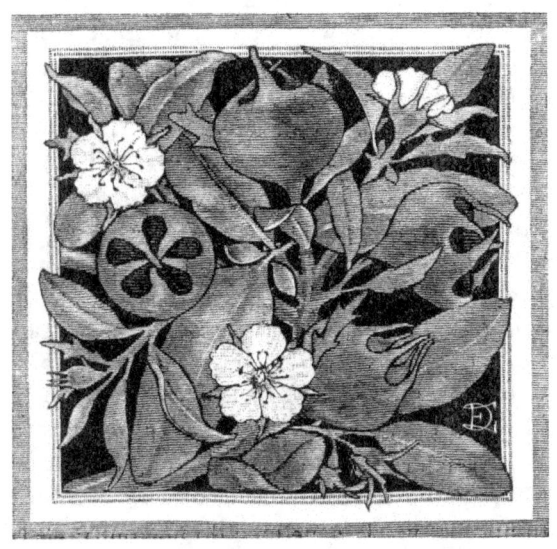

Treatment of Medlar, more Modern than Gothic

influence of Greek, Gothic, and Chinese ornament ; the medlar panel above is composed something in the manner of English Gothic ; but in neither of them is there any thought of imitation. The days are past in which men worked in the manner traditional to their craft, knowing no other. We

have no traditions, excepting perhaps those of the
particular workshop in which our apprenticeship
was served ; and we soon learn that these are not
as the laws of the Medes and Persians.

We are perplexed at the very beginning by
the thought of what style we shall adopt. One
authority declares with confidence that Gothic is
the only true and living style, another is equally
certain that the one and only worthy aim in art is
Classic perfection ; one suggests that we should put
our trust in Eastern art, another deifies the Renaissance ; and there are equally fervent apostles of the
Jacobean and the later French schools. The very
multitude of voices suggests the truth, that not one
of these ancient styles is quite suited to our time.
Some of them are worn rather threadbare, and of
those that are still serviceable it is not possible that
any one will fit our every modern want and fancy.
The very assertion of an universal fitness, reminds
us rather too forcibly of those omnipotent medicines
that are advertised to cure anything, from an ache
to an apoplexy. If sane men do not put their faith
in a particular pill, and believe that it is equally
efficacious against all ailments, still less should they
blindly swallow the nostrum that one particular
style of bygone art will answer all our present
purposes.

Nearly all old work has something to teach us,
but the more deeply we study it the more
thoroughly shall we realise that side by side with

the particular merits of each style lie its particular
defects. The grace which we find wanting in one
style is atoned for by a strength and character
which are absent from the other. One excels in
form, another in colour, a third is symbolic, and a
fourth sensuous ; each is best in some particular,
even though its individual excellence may not be of
a very high order.

It would be beyond the truth to say that the
principles which underlie all old work are the same.
Those principles are as diverse as the temperaments
and characters of the races among whom they were
developed. The Egyptians loved mystery and
symbolism ; the Greeks carried the refinement of
form to perfection ; the Romans revelled in richness ; the Byzantines indulged in a brilliance of
colour that is yet always barbaric ; the Arabs
gave themselves up to the subtle interweaving of
intricate detail ; the artists of the Gothic period
combined religious sentiment with energy of execution ; and those of the Renaissance returned to the
worship of beauty for its own sake. We should
seek in vain elsewhere for the all-pervading symbolism that runs through Egyptian ornament, the
purity of line that characterises Greek detail, or
the sumptuousness that belongs to Roman scrollery.
Inasmuch as all nations and all ages differ, their
expression in ornament differs ; and inasmuch as all
nations and all ages are alike, they express themselves alike in their every-day art.

Though one race of men may be naturally disposed to remain in the grooves of tradition, and another always eager to start off on a new track, there is no race of men among whom all are exactly alike; everywhere there have been skilful and clumsy, conscientious and dishonest workmen, and in every period of art there has been good work and bad.

Fortunately for us, the latter has most of it gone the way of bad work and perished; so that, although in ancient art collectively we have not, as in Nature, an unerring guide, it is mainly the good that remains to us. The winnowing of old work has been done for us by the sure hand of Time.

The art of design does not consist in the slavish reproduction of classic, mediæval, or other ornamental detail. It is not enough that we are familiar with antique forms, we must make ourselves masters of the old methods, that we too may go and do, not likewise, but as good or better, if we can. Our success is more than uncertain, and, to speak frankly, we must admit that few of us are likely to approach the perfection of the best old work; but if we rely upon copyism our failure is inevitable. Yet surely a doubtful success is to be preferred to certain failure. Slavish work is always lifeless work, and a copy is after all only a copy. Art should be studied by artists in the spirit in which Bacon said that books should be read, "not to Contradict and Confute; Nor to Beleeve and Take for granted;

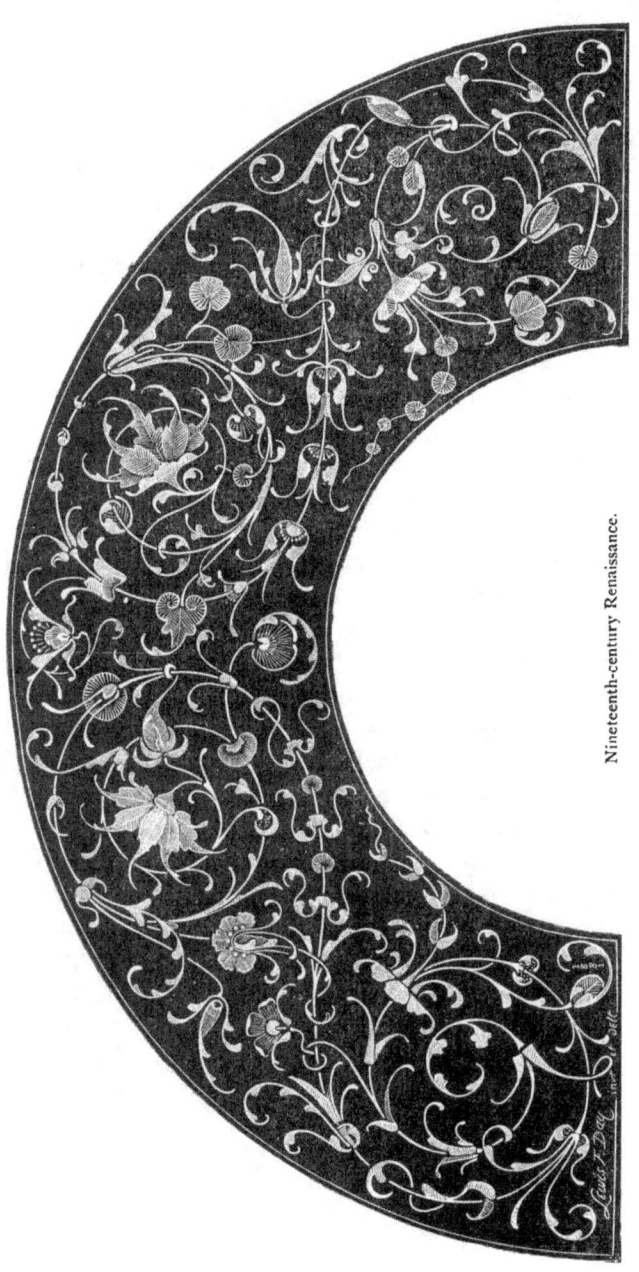

Nineteenth-century Renaissance.

Nor to Finde Talke and Discourse; but to weigh and Consider." Like books, too, some ornament is only "to be Tasted." No great good can come of *swallowing* old work whole; it is certain that whatever of it we take should "be Chewed and Digested."

By all means let us study old work, and that earnestly; but do not let us be greedy over it. Many an archæologically-minded designer (if reproduction may be called design) has before now suffered from a surfeit of old examples which it was hopelessly impossible for him to digest. What wonder if the productions of such a one have all the monstrous inconsistency of a nightmare! Archæology is a study in itself, and one that is of considerable assistance to the artist; but it is not art, nor will it serve as a substitute for it. Individuals may affect a particular period of ancient art, but most men feel the absurdity of attempting to resuscitate among us to-day the ornament of any other time or people. What if it be the art of Egypt, in its rigid stateliness; of Greece, in its monotonous perfection; of Rome, with its dangerous richness? What if it be Byzantine or Gothic ornament, earnest but bigoted; Mohammedan design, as exquisite as it is limited? What if it be of old Japan, with its facility not always restrained by taste; of the Renaissance, that is responsible for the most beautiful and the most degraded in decorative art ? In no case is it possible that such art can be sufficiently in sympathy with us to serve our needs of every day. The recent reaction against the pedantry of modern Gothicism was but natural.

Men were so sick of trying to build nine-teenth - century dwel-ling - houses according to the pre-cedent of thirteenth-century churches and abbeys, that even the affecta-tion of what is called "Queen Anne" architecture

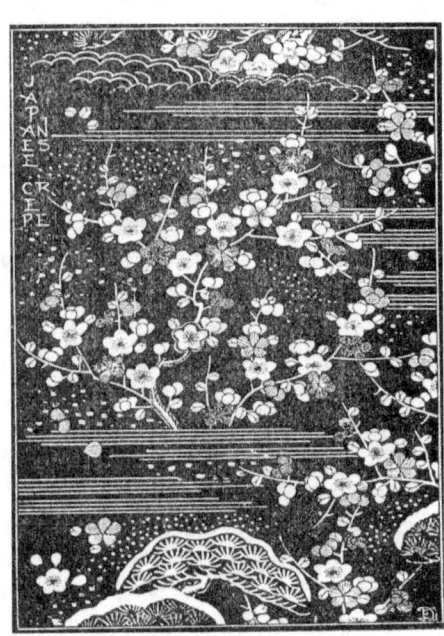

Japanese ornament.

was welcome, because, being really a sort of no-style-in-particular, it allowed some freedom to the artist. The promptitude with which that liberty has been used is an indication, perhaps, of a temper to which a fusion of past styles into something like really characteristic modern work, may not be altogether impossible.

Although each style of ancient art has its intrinsic merit, the value of any particular style is relative, and depends upon our immediate object in study. We should not expect to find in an old Egyptian mummy-case any very marvellous degree of airy grace or elegance, nor look for quaintness and piquancy in the sculptures of the Parthenon; we should not go back to ancient Rome for purity of style, nor to Byzantium for beauty of figure-drawing; we do not expect to find freedom in Moorish art, or restraint in Japanese. If the experience of time past is to serve our turn, according to the nature of our own work we must refer to the art of the particular period or people that afforded the most perfect examples of that kind; according to our particular difficulty we should refer to the particular style of art in which it had been most satisfactorily solved. Notwithstanding the beauty of a great deal of old work (and some of it is so perfect that the mere study of its details is a sort of education in itself), there is infinitely more to be learnt from the study of ancient processes than from the worship of antique forms. Half the charm of a design vanishes at once when we discover that it is only a reflection of something better that is past and dead. We grow tired of the continual repetition of the same beautiful but long since lifeless forms. On the contrary, our respect for the consummate art, the admirable tact, the masterly treatment of material, that we find in the best old work, can but increase with closer familiarity ; here indeed we have something that is not only worthy of study, but capable of impregnating our work with no little of its own reality and manliness.

It must be confessed that we have made no very wise use of the abundant wealth of old work now so easily accessible to us all. For the most part we have simply abused the opportunities of study : we have been content to copy the handwriting of the past without attempting to decipher the meaning of the message it conveys to us. With all our boasted knowledge, we are ignorant of what is best worth knowing in the past. Not that we are so dull and stupid as would seem, not that we are simply lazy, but that we are in such haste—haste to outstrip our fellows, haste to reach notoriety, haste to make money,—that we snatch at what is obvious, and have no time to seek beneath the surface for what is best worth having.

The good that modern decoration has derived from the accumulation of examples of ancient art around us in this generation, is out of all proportion small to what it should and would have been, if we had made intelligent use of them. Manufacturers reproduce at preposterous prices laborious copies of inexpen-

sive oriental pottery, which is chiefly admirable for
the ease and directness with which the artist potter
produced so satisfactory a result ; while they
remain in contented ignorance of the secrets of the
superiority of Eastern ware to the products of
Staffordshire. In spite of the influx of Japanese art
among us, in spite of common-sense almost, they
still hold the faith of the most ignorant amateurs,
that finish is only so much smoothness, that the
highest art consists in the most minute elaboration.
They think to imitate Etruscan terra-cotta by
copying antique vase shapes, and *printing* upon
them mechanical travesties of the bold and beautiful
forms that flowed from the brush of the Greek so
freely, that it is difficult to say exactly how
much of the credit is due to the artist and how
much to the brush. It is the same in almost everything. We copy the patterns of Persian carpets,
while we somehow miss the charm of their colour.
In all our modern Gothic furniture, where shall we
find the simple but effective carving, clean, crisp,
and vigorous, that enriched, almost as a matter of
course, the common oak chests of two or three
centuries ago ? We should not dare to do so little
to a panel as the old craftsmen felt to be enough.
Yet the flat carving of the panel on page 39 is
sufficient to be decorative. That it is not beautiful
is the fault of mediæval German art.

There is perplexity in the wonderful variety of

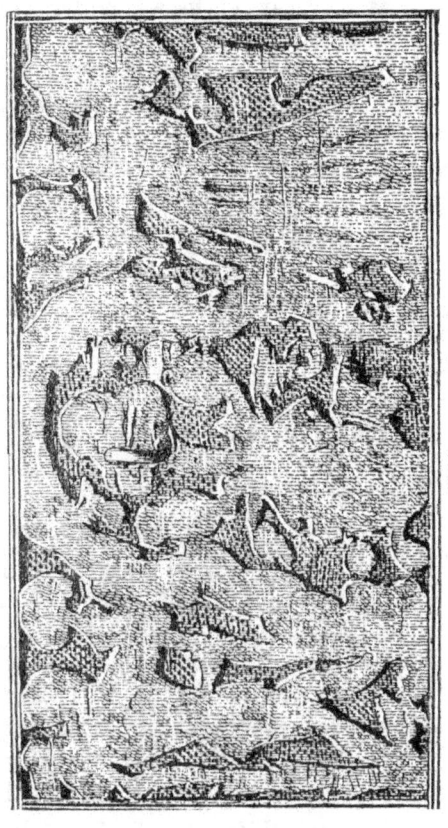

Old German wood-carving.

the styles of art with which we are familiar, but there is something more than perplexity : each reflects some light on the other. With all the difference between different styles of ancient ornament, there are certain characteristics common to the best, of whatever race or period. A critical examination of old work will go far to show that the best in each style is akin to what is best in all others ; even as its authors, though they differ in type and feature as Chinaman differs from Greek, are all built upon the skeleton common to humanity. And as all races go to make mankind, all styles go to make ornament, embodying the unwritten laws of decorative design. Not that they were ever consciously followed by the artists. The grammar is compiled from the language; the language is not constructed on the lines of the grammar. Nevertheless, what is to be gathered from the practice of the masters of design may be formulated for the guidance of beginners. All arbitrary rules and dogmas are in the nature of leading-strings, irritating to a degree when once we can do without them; but small children cannot run alone, and every one is a child in art to begin with.

Of modern ornament the most perfect is that which is not modern, that is to say, such Indian, Persian, Japanese or other Eastern art, as is traditional, and has changed little or not at all during centuries.

All that we know about the ornament of the future is that it will be influenced by what has gone before. What that influence will be is matter of speculation. When we think of the diversity between ancient and modern modes of life and thought, we cannot but feel that the expression of ancient and modern art must indeed be different. Yet, when we come to reflect how near we are to the most remote of our race, and how little of novelty

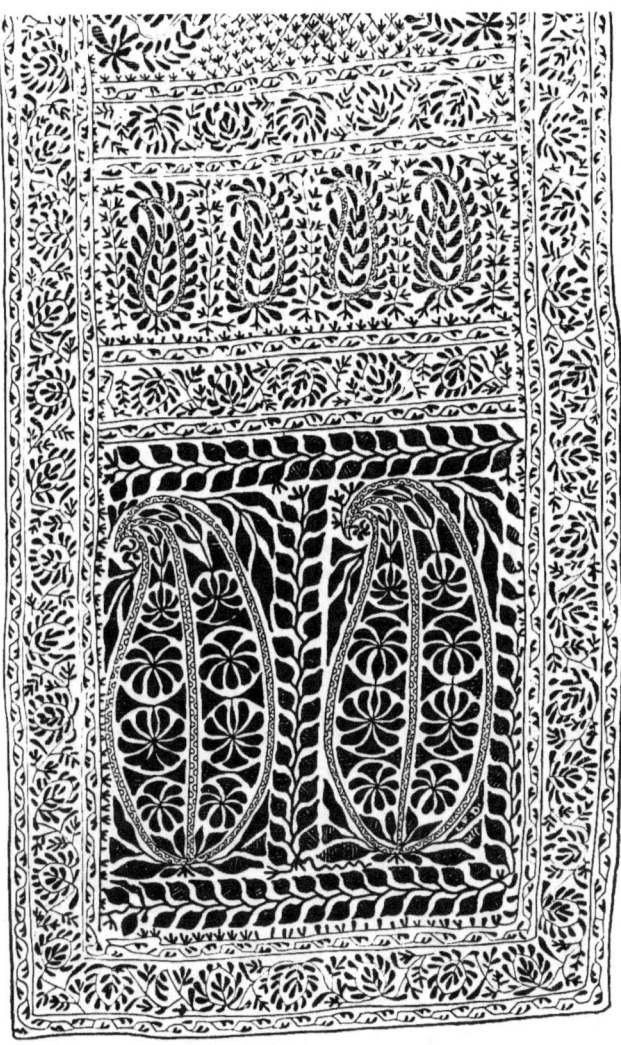

Modern traditional ornament.

there is in art, we are more disposed to believe that the elements of all possible art lie buried in the ruins of what has been.

The past is there to teach us, the present is here to work in. It is a question no less difficult than important to the designer : what is the relation of ancient precedent to modern practice ?

THE NATURE OF ART.

"Art is man's nature."

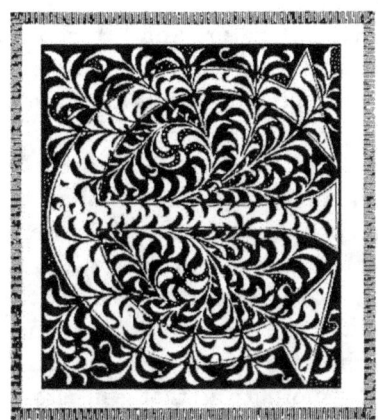

VERY day fresh ink is shed in the war that is perpetually waging between the followers of Nature on the one side and of Art on the other. May be the words are only so much waste of energy. There have been graver battles to as little purpose since the world began. May be the combatants, like other and more deadly adversaries, are warring under the universal banner of misapprehension, each in truth fighting against the other for much the same idea, called by a different name.

Though art is not another name for nature, artists, even the most opposed, will admit that in nature lies the source of art. The difference of opinion is as to the use or abuse of nature, as to the lesson to be learnt from her, the one school maintaining that the whole secret of art lies in strict fidelity to fact, the other seeking to subject all art to the bondage of a narrow conventionality. The obstinacy of each party is encouraged by the adherence of the other to its own dogma ; and both fallacies are the more invincible through the alloy of truth that is in both.

The relative positions of nature and art depend very materially upon the nature of the art in question. Painter and decorator represent the two extremes of art, and there is no more prolific source of confusion than to identify one with the other.

The art of Michael Angelo, and indeed of all the great Italians of the Renaissance, was all more or less decorative ; painter and decorator may be said to meet in them ; but it is only on the summit of art that the pictorial and the decorative join hands. One may start with the idea of painting a picture, and end by making it conform to all that is necessary to decoration. Or one may begin with a decorative scheme, and carry it to the furthest point of pictorial perfection. Parnassus may be climbed from different sides ; and a man is painter or decorator, not according to the height he may have reached, but according to the side from which he set out.

There is always the broad distinction between realism and idealism in art, and in decoration it is more distinct than ever. It is not that the adherents of either theory deny the value and necessity of

nature to art. The question is not whether ornament should be natural or artificial, but : what
is the natural way of treating ornament ? what is
the artistic way of rendering nature ? It may be
assumed that no one seriously believes that art is
nature, and that nature is art. However dependent
the one may be upon the other, they are always
distinctly two. Nature is before all art, and above
it, and beyond. All that gives us satisfaction in
ornament existed first of all in nature, though not
of necessity in the animal or vegetable kingdom.
Human nature counts for something. We have
long since ceased to be the unsophisticated children
of nature. Art may be only *second* nature, but it is
a very real one to us ; and the discussion of human
affairs from the point of view of primeval simplicity,
however interesting, is scarcely practical.

The world has determined that it cannot do
without ornament, and if it be contrary to nature,
nature, in so far as it is refractory, must be brought
into subjection. Is not our whole life artificial ?
Whosoever takes service under the banner of art
must keep in the ranks. To say that it is art which
should serve under nature, is to say that ornament
has no business to exist ; for ornament very clearly
insists upon the precedence of art.

In the case of easel pictures it is different. The
painter is restrained only within the limits of his
own ability and the four sides of his picture frame.
The decorator has comparatively little liberty of

Adaptation of seaweed to ornament.

invention, and yet no excuse for the lack of it. He can put in no plea for unreasoning realism. His business is to add the grace of ornament to something predetermined, if not already in existence; and the opportunity for naturalism is of the rarest occurrence. He may not say all that he could say. He has not even the privilege of silence. His art is, so to speak, in submission to one continual cross-examination. Whatever he does is more or less in answer to the question : how in this instance can art and beauty best be reconciled ? His rank as a decorator will depend upon his habitual success in the solution of that problem.

The copying of natural forms is no solution, but an evasion, of the difficulty. If we would pay to Nature that sincerest flattery of imitation, we should begin by adapting, as she inevitably would do, every form that we adopt from her to our immediate purpose. That so-called ornament which is only a copy of nature is no more natural than it is workmanlike or intelligent. Ornament is in its nature an accessory art, and must, in common-sense, be reduced to harmony with the architecture, craft, or industry with which it is associated.

We misjudge whatever we judge by a false standard, whether it be painting, to which we do injustice by comparing it with nature, or decorative art, by confounding it with pictorial. Judge ornament after its kind, consider it as ornament, and you cannot fail to see that its most essential characteristic is fitness.

There are persons to whom the necessary adaptation of natural forms to ornamental conditions is incomprehensible. It is not long since a painter, whose own work is characterised by taste, took occasion publicly to stigmatise this adaptation as "a stopping short." It may be so. Sculpture is, no doubt, a stopping short of colour, music a stopping short of words, poetry a stopping short of reality ; and like them decorative art, too, stops short. But it would indicate a truer appreciation of the different arts to say, rather, that this apparent "stopping short" is really selection, a deliberate and wise rejection of the unnecessary colour, form, reality, in favour of the all-important harmony or impression to be produced. Ornament may be called, if you will, a stopping short of imitation, as

breadth a stopping short of detail. All art stops
short of nature, and that intentionally; else we
should have no drawings in black and white, no
sculpture that stopped short of colour, no paintings
stopping short of absolute relief. Waxwork would
be our ideal; and, with the aid of clockwork,
no need even to stop short of motion. Science
and art might eventually be coupled indeed,
instead of, as now, only on the headings of news-
papers. What a prospect opens itself before us,
ending in a vision—Art yielding at length to the
fond embrace of Mechanism!

Art is compromise. The most literal of painters
rejects many truths for the sake of the one truth he
desires to enforce. Children and amateurs attempt
to represent all that is before them. The painter
makes up his mind what effect it is that he wishes
to produce and sacrifices all else to that. So does
the decorator. But the sacrifices due from him to
purpose, place, material, and fitness, are greater. He
has to choose, not between beauty and truth, but
between one truth and another, and all that is
contrary to his decorative purpose it is his business
to suppress. Half the art of the decorator is in the
faculty of selection. It is not so easy to strike
a balance between beauty and use. Let any
painter who may amuse himself by condescending
to decoration, attempt, by the process of "stopping
short," to produce a decorative work. Perhaps he
will realise, after inevitable failure, that to reach

the success that seemed so easy he must retrace his steps, and travel quite a different path—difficult in proportion to its unfamiliarity.

The decorative treatment of natural forms consists neither in the violation nor in the disregard of them, but in their selection and adaptation. If familiarity with nature offer some temptation to the ornamentist, it adds, if he can only exercise restraint upon himself, and use without abusing his knowledge, immeasurably to his power. Natural details should not be left out through ignorance, but deliberately rejected. To be ignorant of nature is to miss the most fruitful source of suggestion, the most perfect and most constant illustration of fitness in treatment. What has been called a conventional treatment of floral form is too often more like a diagram than a design. There is neither art nor nature in the grouping of any number of copies of the same prim sprig of foliage round a central point, like so many spokes of a floral wheel. To dissect a plant and arrange its members on a geometric basis, is a somewhat childish idea of ornament. Dissection is useful enough in its way, but is only a preparatory study.

The illustrations overleaf show a study of an apple bough, selected examples of the growth of the tree, and the adaptation of these forms to the purpose of an inlaid panel.

It behoves the ornamentist not only to study nature, but to be on the look-out for those natural

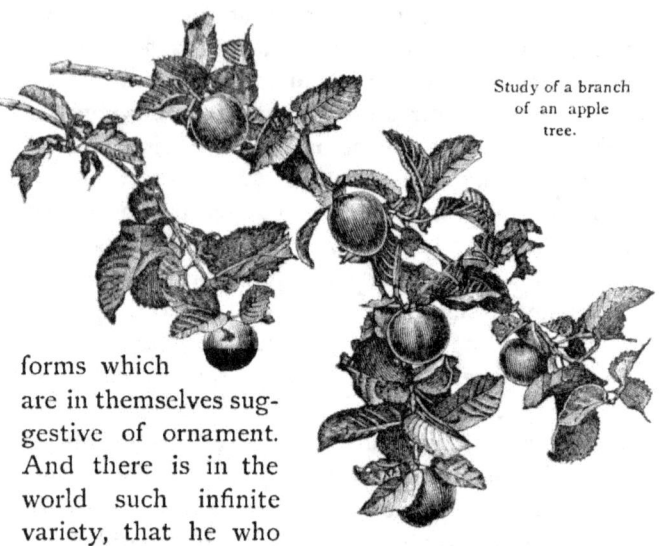

Study of a branch
of an apple
tree.

forms which
are in themselves sug-
gestive of ornament.
And there is in the
world such infinite
variety, that he who
needs must cling always to nature's skirts has
scarce occasion to let go his hold.   Not seldom it
will be found that the characteristic features of a
plant, for example, are at the same time the most
ornamental ; so that, in adapting it to ornamental
design, he may emphasise instead of obliterating
its individuality.

So essentially ornamental is the growth of some
plants, that a closer study of nature shows how many
a decorative detail which we have been in the habit
of looking upon as evidence of consummate skill
in design, is in reality borrowed from nature.

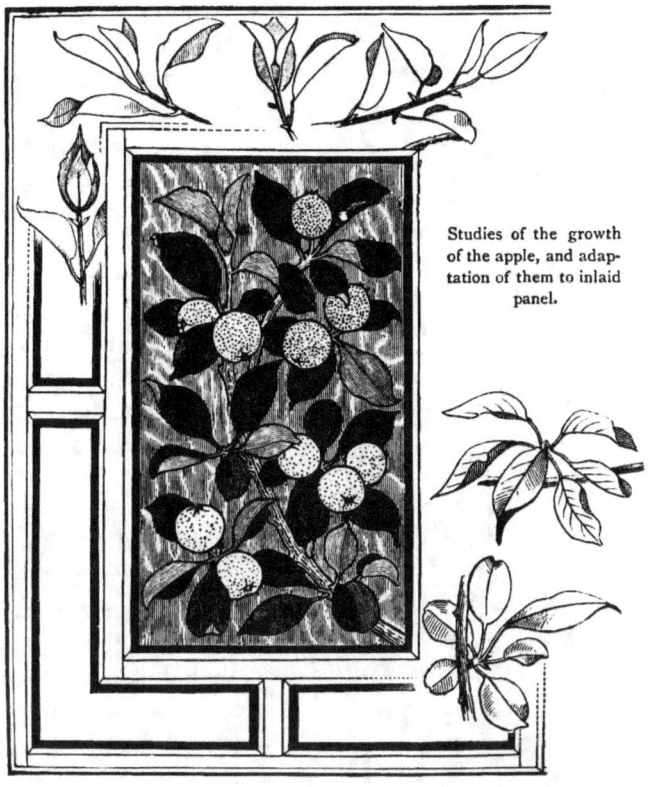

Studies of the growth of the apple, and adaptation of them to inlaid panel.

In the same way, when we come to adapt a study from nature to the purposes of design, we often find that we have, all unconsciously, reproduced some quite familiar form of ornament.

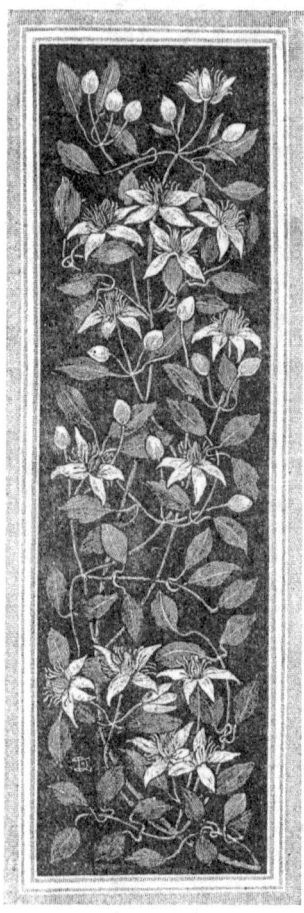

Clematis panel.

Not only is every particular part of a plant suggestive of decoration, but each different species reveals fresh decorative possibilities. Certain plants grow with such crispness and vigour in the curl of their foliage, that they almost invite the smith to hammer his metal like that! Some are as broad and large in style as if they were already carved in stone; and others, again, grow in such symmetrical and simple lines, that they all but say to the decorator in so many words, "Come, copy us!"

It is almost a wonder that it is not a common practice to inlay panels with the representation of autumn foliage ; it suggests itself so obviously for the purpose.

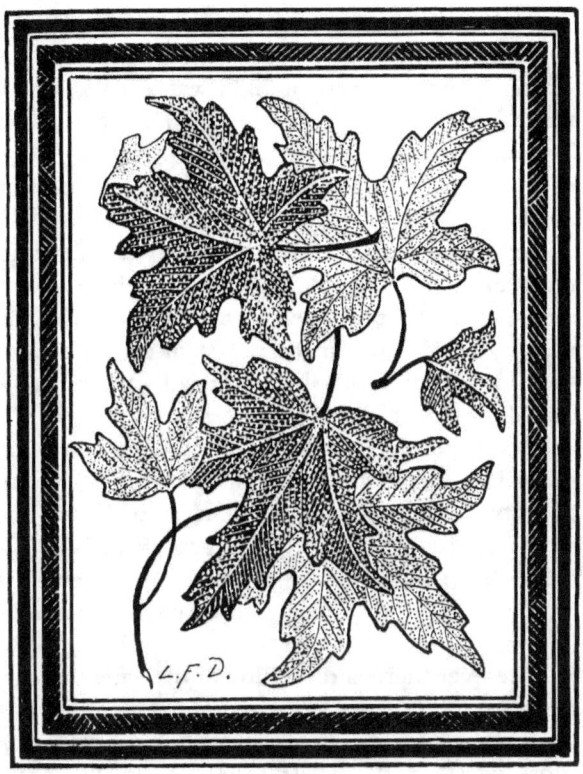

Panel of autumn leaves.

The best Japanese work is an instance in answer

to the question as to how far one may go with safety in the direction of imitative ornament. The limit of natural treatment in design is not marked by a hard line separating ornament from all that is pictorial in art : there is no fixed boundary anywhere, only, as it were, a high-water mark, beyond which the tide of nature seldom dares to rise. There are cases in which imitation may be carried as far as you please, so long as it neither obtrudes itself nor brings into obtrusive prominence the object ornamented. The thing to be decorated must always be in the artist's thoughts. If for a moment he be perverted from his decorative purpose by the delight in the power of copying nature, the probability is that his work will distract attention from the object it professes to ornament to itself; or, perhaps, draw to it more notice than is becoming. The nearer the ornamentist ventures to nature, the greater his danger of falling into the vulgarity of making his art obtrusive. One must be sparing of imitative ornament, the more sparing the closer the imitation comes to nature.

Wherever there is repetition of ornamental forms, it is essential that the natural element in them be toned down to the necessary key and made subsidiary to art. If this be a kind of treason against nature, it is a treason of which all of us are guilty when we cook our food before eating it. The degree of cooking necessarily varies with the

circumstances ; but it may safely be said that the
more frequently a pattern is repeated, the more
imperative it is that it should be thoroughly "well
done." The best carpets, for instance, are the
Persian, Indian, and Turkey—and all the nature
has been pretty well cooked out of their design :
they are the very reverse of naturalistic.

Nothing is more becoming in ornament than
modesty. It is that kind of design which most
prides itself upon being natural, which is most apt
to "o'erstep the modesty of nature." One would
have fancied that the necessity for some adaptation
of nature to ornamental purposes needed only to be
fairly stated in order to be accepted once and for
all. But the principle of propriety in ornament
has found little acceptance in practice. Men may
fairly be judged by the literature current among
them. That of the moment may convict us of an
affected interest in decorative art ; that of a few
years ago shows, even when the writer was a man
of culture, scarce a trace of a taste in design.
Leigh Hunt enlivened his prison walls with a
paper in imitation of a trellis of roses, and Byron
was charmed with the effect. One would have
thought that the prison was bad enough without
the wall-paper ! Of more recent writers Charles
Reade makes his Margaret van Eyck exceeding
wroth at the flat treatment of illuminations common
in the fifteenth century. She ends by taking the
brush from her pupil's hand and proceeding " to

shade her fruit and reptiles a colour false in nature,
but true relatively to that monstrous ground of
glaring gold; and in five minutes out came a
bunch of raspberries, stalk and all, and a'most flew
into your mouth." Surely that is just what the
illuminator should have avoided. One would have
been inclined to credit an artist who had the tact
to use "a colour false in nature, but true relatively,"
with wit enough to keep her raspberries within
bounds. If one of the author's characters were
accused of walking out of his pages, it might not
appear to him to be the highest possible praise
of his work as art.

It would be easy to multiply instances of the
popular innocence, a generation ago, of the fact
that there was any necessity whatever for restraint
in ornamental design. And until quite recently, it
would have been hard to find in modern literature
any hint of a taste cultivated in this direction;
whilst there are instances of a preference for what
is florid and ill-judged abounding in the writings
even of men in other respects cultivated.

An "inimitable" author shows singular capacity
for misunderstanding the gist of the whole matter.
In a caricature of the early days of the Government
Schools of Art, an examiner is made to say : " You
are not to have in any object of use or ornament
what would be contradiction in fact. You don't
walk about on flowers in fact, you cannot be allowed
to walk upon flowers in carpets; you don't find

that foreign birds and butterflies come and perch
upon your crockery; you never meet quadrupeds
going up and down walls; you must not have
quadrupeds presented on walls." This may serve
to raise a laugh, fulfilling in so far its purpose; but
Dickens should have known better than that. What
he says amounts to nothing; it does not touch the
point at all. The foreign birds and butterflies are
no more obnoxious than would be the common
sparrow or the "meadow-brown" that might happen
to settle upon a teacup. The flowers that over-
sprawl the lodging-house carpet are in bad taste
because of their obtrusiveness; they are uninteresting because they show so little purpose or intelligence on the part of the designer; they are inartistic
because they travesty in a coarse and clumsy
manner the delicate forms and colouring of nature;
they are offensive altogether because, if they could
reproduce the beauty of nature, they would be unfit
for us to walk upon, unfit for the subordinate place
they occupy, quite unfit, in short, for every purpose
of a carpet.

It is not merely the representation of things that
would themselves be out of place that is objectionable. It is the imitation that is out of place. A
china flower-vase in imitation of wickerwork is not
more contemptible than a dessert-dish which consists of vine-leaves modelled in majolica. The fact
that the basket would not hold water, and that the
natural vine-leaves might serve very well for an

impromptu dish, does not alter the case. It is necessary to distinguish clearly what is wrong in these imitative tricks, and why it is wrong. The examples mentioned above are doubly in fault. In the first place, it is surely unreasonable to make a vase after the model of a basket, or to fashion a dish in the likeness of a leaf. In the second, it is unworkmanlike to manipulate porcelain as if it were osiers, or earthenware as if it did not more readily lend itself to forms as beautiful as that of any leaf is inappropriate. For it is an inflexible law of design that in every work of decorative art the artist should be influenced by two distinct considerations, namely, by the purpose of the thing to be decorated, and by the characteristic qualities of the material in which he is working. To design, as in the two instances supposed, without regard to either consideration, is to confess one's incapacity, and to confess it twice over.

The least reference to the laws of nature would suggest a very different procedure. Every tree that grows adapts itself to its place, or dies in the attempt. When the circumstances of an individual plant are changed, nature modifies the habits of that plant to suit its altered state. If a flower that is naturally short in the stalk, with its leaves clustered closely round it, chance to grow among tall shrubs that overshadow it, it will shoot up so quickly, in haste to get its share of the sunlight, that it will leave long lengths of stalk between the leaves, quite contrary to its habitual growth. Again, the leaves of the ivy grow in spiral order round the stem, but against a wall they appear alternately upon it ; and the rooty fibres by which it attaches itself, do not occur on the branches of the ivy when it has ceased to creep, and holds up its head among the trees.

Nature brings forth herbs and flowers that answer all manner of human needs ; but her scope, apparently, does not include the art of decoration. Had she produced a species of plants whose province in the world was to serve as models for painter, carver, or weaver, she would doubtless have modified her accustomed forms and colours to meet this novel purpose. Since she has neglected to do this, it devolves, obviously, upon us to adapt whatever we may take from nature to the purpose of our art.

Even the painter cannot afford to transcribe too literally from nature. There is imminent danger that in a painting the colours of nature will be too startlingly bright, even though they be less intense than in the reality. But grass in spring is never too green for us ; soft cloud-shadows creep over it continually, and its most vivid colour is only revealed in momentary gleams of sunlight, too bright to last. "Why is it that you have made me so perishable ?" asked Beauty of Jupiter, and the god answered : "Nay, but it is only the Perishable that I have endowed with beauty !" Certainly the

most beautiful effects are those that are most
fleeting. To fix them before us in naked isolation,
is to rob them of their loveliness. They decline
to be transplanted bodily. It takes a poet
to translate them to a sphere higher than their
own.

"True to nature" is the catchword of a party.
In art the most essential truth is truth to your
purpose, truth to the end in view. In ornament
we have rather to consider the nature of the work
to be done, than the nature of any object from
which we may gather an idea. If our intention
be purely decorative, the mere fact that nature
has suggested a certain form, need not trammel
us in the use of it. We are perfectly at liberty to
depart from the suggestive type if we see fit, or
even to engraft upon it a character derived from
quite another source, so long as we can persuade
all into harmony, and so produce consistent and
satisfactory ornament. Where, however, the natural
type has been selected for the sake of symbolism
or suggestion, one is scarcely at liberty to alter
anything that is characteristic ; certainly nothing
should be added arbitrarily to it, and what is
omitted should only be as a sacrifice to the
necessities of material, position, or purpose. For
example, if in a decorative panel we wished to
symbolise Morning by the " *Day's eye*," we should
not be justified in disregarding any of the characteristics of the particular form of daisy that we

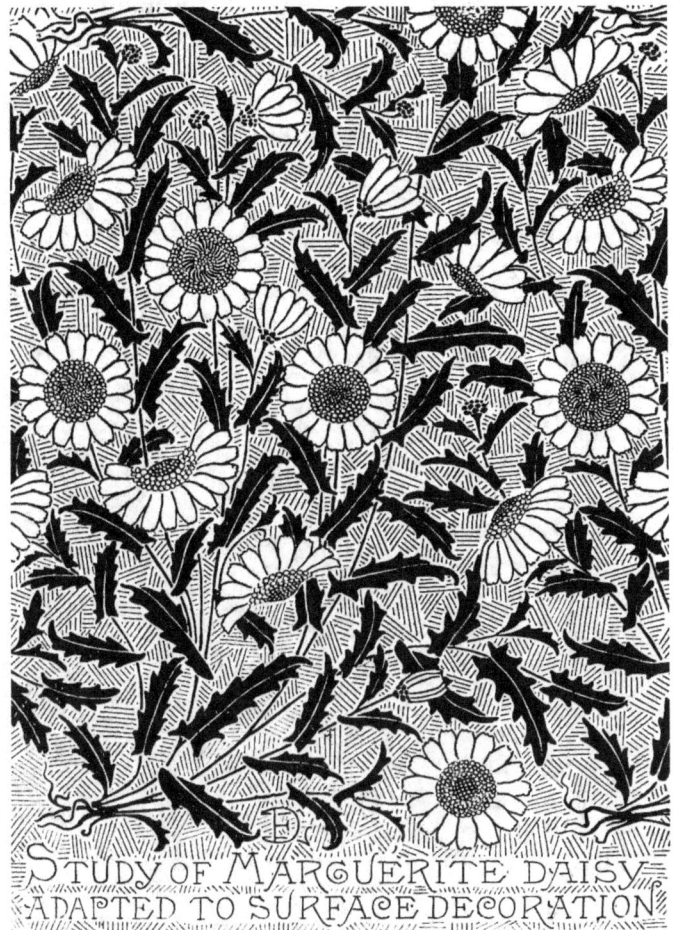

STUDY OF MARGUERITE DAISY
ADAPTED TO SURFACE DECORATION

might choose for that purpose. It would be desirable to consider the growth as well as the form of the flower, and, indeed, due modification would consist in little more than in fitting it to the space it occupied, and in treating it according to the nature of wood-carving, modelling, painting, or whatever process we might adopt for its execution. In adapting the same plant to surface decoration, as in a textile fabric or wall paper, the necessity for repetition, and for a somewhat uniform distribution of design, would

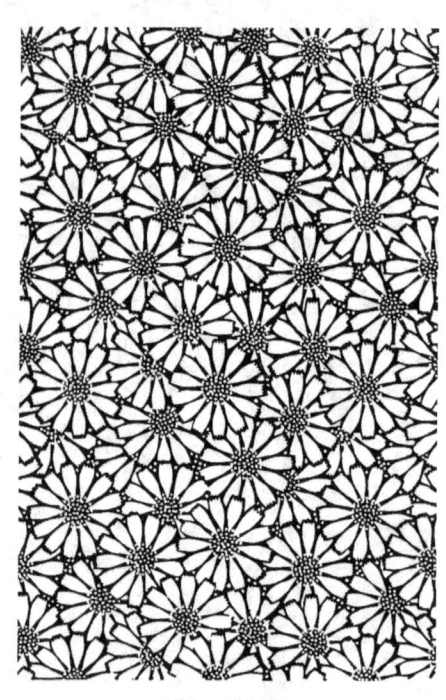

Diaper of daisies.

necessitate less strict adherence to natural growth ; and the consideration of the secondary nature of all mere surface decoration would suggest a flatter treatment. The design might even consist of the flowers alone, without any indication of growth. If it were only the shape of the flower itself that led to its use, and no value were attached to its meaning, it might be modified out of all recognition ; and every departure from nature would be justified by the production of beautiful ornament. There is a wide difference between ornament that has been suggested by a natural type, and natural form used for its own sake, but reduced to harmony with some ornamental scheme or purpose.

The fittest representation of any plant in ornament will be attained by comparing the thing itself

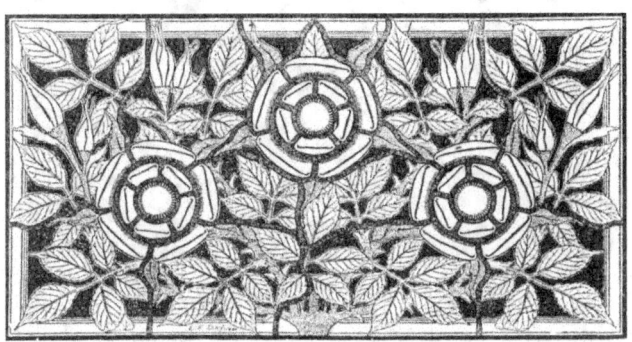

Adaptation of Tudor rose to stained glass.

in nature with its various representations in the art of the past, having always special reference to

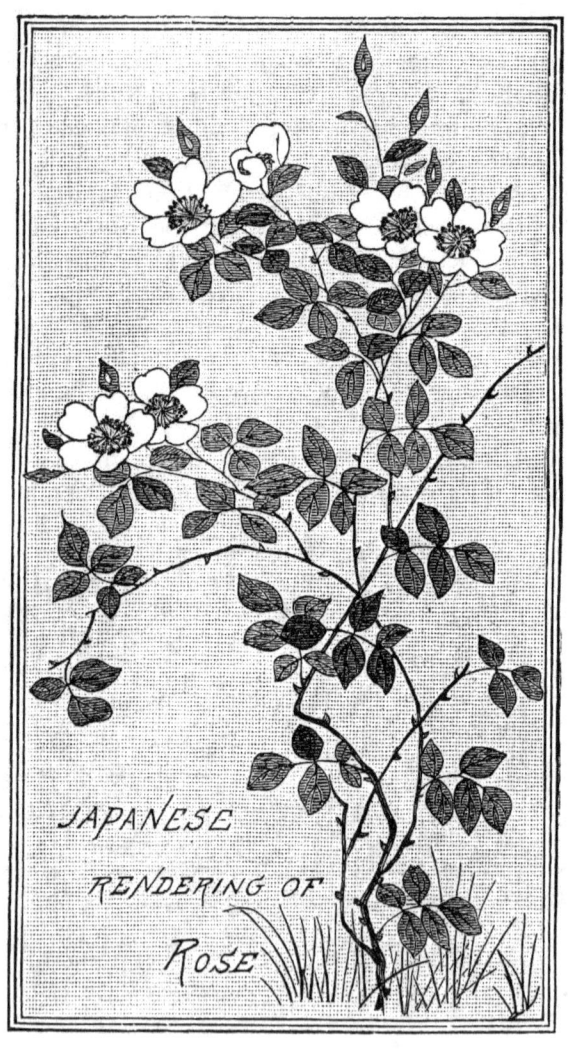

the immediate purpose in hand. Compare the rose in your garden with the Tudor version of it, with the Japanese and Persian renderings.

The keynote of a design may be struck by something in the flower itself, or by something in any one of its past representations, or by the material and tools in use ; but the one thing of importance is that all should be in tune.

Nowhere is the discrepancy between idea and execution more obvious than in the work of the heraldic painter of the nineteenth century. His is an art that, in the light of the present day, has rather a dried-up, mummy-like look. It is, to all intents and purposes, more dead than alive. Nevertheless folk do not seem disposed to let it die outright. It lingers yet among us, but in what a form! It is unworthy even of a generation who are proud

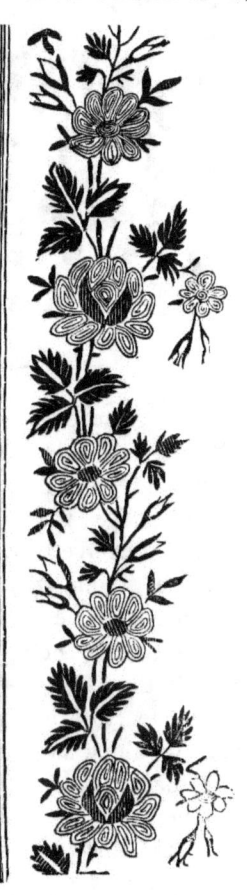

Persian rendering of the rose.

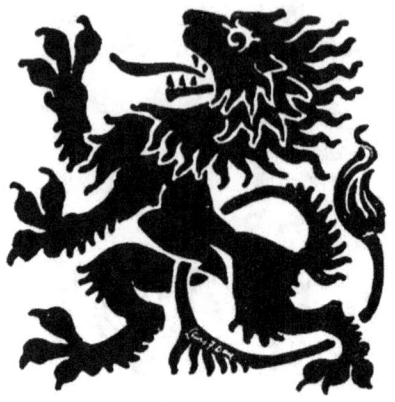

Heraldic Lion.

to display on their trim coach-panels a shield no ancestor of theirs was ever known to bear in war. There is all the difference in the world between " a lion gules " and our " red lion." The mediæval herald was not guilty of the absurdity of representing a zoological beast dyed red. He concerned himself little about the anatomy of a natural lion ; he sought to symbolise the bravery, the lion-like nature, as he conceived it, of some fierce combatant ; and he managed to combine symbolism with ornament. The forms he drew were sufficiently intelligible for their purpose, and more so perhaps than if they had been more literal. There would be no fear of mistaking his device in the field. Such heraldry as this was heraldic, thorough-bred. It remained for a more cultivated age than his to generate a mongrel something between heraldry and the illustrations in a natural history book. " But," says the Philistine, " if you want a lion paint a lion, and not a nondescript creature that might with quite as much propriety be called a leopard or a cat!" Yes, if that is what you want! But heraldry has to do with symbols, not pictures. Then paint the symbol. A zoological lion is as much out of place on a shield of arms as an heraldic beast would be in the wilds of Africa.

A lion may be, and doubtless is, formed as to his anatomy much as Sir Edwin Landseer represented him. He may, after

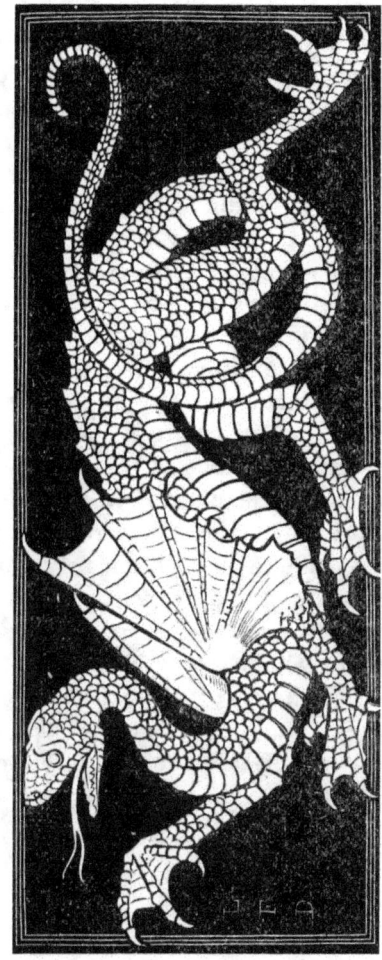

Heraldic Dragon.

a full meal, or when he is sentimentally disposed,
put on such an expression of silly satisfaction as
greets us, four times over, in the countenances of
the lions in Trafalgar Square. But is that the
British lion? Then he is tamed indeed! What
right has such a beast to pose at the base of
Nelson's column? Does he symbolise the pluck of
Nelson, or the sovereignty of Nelson's country?
He is about as appropriate there as a rhinoceros
would be, or a gorilla; a crocodile would have been
infinitely more suggestive.

It is in a little art like this of heraldry that the
reasonableness of apt expression is most obvious ;
but it is not the less reasonable where it is less
evident. In all art that has any claim to be
decorative the natural must needs be translated into the language of that art. The decorative is the
vernacular. Though our art be but the expression
of nature, it is a "conscious utterance," by which is
meant something more than a parrot cry. The
artist's whole strength is in his loyalty to nature ;
not in mere verbal fidelity, but in truth—truth to
himself, and to his own highest aims. To the expression of this deeper truthfulness many names
have been given. The artist is content to call it
art.

THE USE IN ORNAMENT.

" Surely use alone
Makes money not a contemptible stone.'

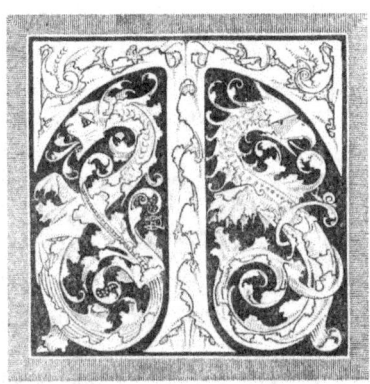

HE arts may be likened to so many languages, more or less akin but never identical, and all of them differing from the utterance of nature. Each of these languages may be said to embrace a variety of dialects ; and the various crafts which go to make decorative art, express themselves most readily in the dialect peculiar to them. If the same idea be expressed in different arts, in each case the form of expression will be different ; and if an artist borrow a notion from some neighbouring craft, he will translate it (as he would if he had borrowed it from nature) into his own language. Art, inasmuch as it implies something more than literal transcript, depends upon expression. All that is asked of the decorative artist is, that he also shall express himself idiomatically.

This idiomatic utterance in ornament has been called conventionality. But the term "conventional" is not altogether a happy one. For one thing it is associated in our minds with what is common-place and insincere, and it is not desirable that the art of ornament should be bracketed in men's minds with the oily humbug that keeps the wheels of society rolling. Then again the word, even as applied to ornament, serves to express that which is traditional; and, if we trace it back to its root, it does mean literally that which has been agreed upon by mutual consent. It happens that a large proportion of the ornament that is idiomatic is at the same time traditional, and more or less stereotyped in character; and, as a consequence, the idea of fixedness or familiarity has come to be popularly associated with the word conventional. Yet it is quite possible to have apt expression in ornament which is not in the least according to tradition.

In the very earliest instances of ornament, obedience to the law of use was a matter of course. If a savage carved the handle of his tomahawk, the carving was just sufficient to give him a tighter grip on the weapon; he would take very good care not to cut so deep as to weaken it. There was no danger of his indulging in ornament that at a critical moment might cost him his life. And to this day we find that among ourselves the

only objects *never* overlaid with misplaced ornamentation are weapons, tools, and things of actual
use, where we cannot afford to play the fool and
sacrifice consistency to what we call " effect."

It is strange that the preference for fit ornament
which comes so naturally to savages, is among
Europeans of the present day a sure sign of culture
in art.

Between the simple forms of things suggested
by utility, and the point at which elaboration and
decoration begin seriously to interfere with their
first purpose, there is a very wide range of ornament. No one, it is to be presumed, will deny that
all ornament that does so interfere oversteps its
limit. It is in hitting the exact mean between bald
simplicity and undue enrichment that the difficulty of decoration consists, and there are obvious
reasons why the art of knowing where to stop
is rarer among us to-day than it was among the
artists of Classic, Mediæval, and Renaissance times,
rarer than it is even now among contemporary
nations of the East. We live in an ambitious, or
rather a pretentious, age. The accessory arts are
all hot to start in business on their own account.
What wonder that they come to grief ?

The consideration of use, wherever it occurs in
decoration, over-rules all others. The tyranny of
the main purpose is absolute. Every breach of the
simple law of common sense condemns itself.
There is no excuse for the house that is picturesque

but inconvenient, or the room that is made beautiful at the cost of homeliness. Nor art nor reason justify tables that are unsteady on their legs, chairs that are not comfortable to sit on, fenders that afford neither protection from the fire nor a resting-place for the feet, fancy cupboards that take up much space and yet take in few things, furniture so fine that it needs to be coddled. We could dispense with teapots designed to look lovely and to dribble, flower-vases so graceful as to the neck that there is no room for the stalks of the flowers, curious ink-stands that seem to hold no ink yet contrive at every dip to leave some on the penholder, book-bindings doomed to be soiled by the touch of the first warm hand, pillows stiff with rich embroidery, and handles quaint but hurtful to hold.

The most successful enrichment is frequently suggested by some useful purpose, and so takes its place as a matter of course. Ornament has uses, too, quite independent of art. Plain surfaces are not only tiresomely monotonous, they are in many cases objectionable as well. The slightest soil or scratch, sooner or later inevitable, betrays itself unnecessarily upon an even ground ; and it is only taking Time by his proverbial forelock, to dapple such spaces with a pattern or to scratch them with ornament. How anxious some young housewives are about the polish of the furniture, and what a relief it would be to their minds if the surface were once for all indented with some slight carving !

Those light silk dresses, too, that show the stains so provokingly, if only they were figured how much more serviceable they would be !

The gravest fault of which ornament can be convicted is that of interfering with the use of the object ornamented, and no merit of execution can condone that offence. That ornament should be beautiful is understood ; it is no less essential that it should be apt.

This is no fantastic theory or arbitrary dogma. It is the plain teaching of nature, of old work, and of common sense. Nature works in no simply utilitarian spirit. Most things natural are also beautiful ; and the beauty is perhaps as much another use as the usefulness is, in a sense, a fresh source of beauty. We do not find in nature instances of ornament that is contrary to use. It may be added to usefulness. There is beauty in the golden glow of the cornfield, and in the crisp growth of the vine ; but the grain is not therefore less nutritious, nor the wine wanting in flavour. In many instances we find on investigation that beauty is subservient to some useful purpose ; as in the case of flowers and berries which by the brilliance of their colouring attract the bees and birds. It is only " Nature's journey-man " who is proud of a progeny of monstrous flowers that bear no fruit, and of which none is to be compared, for beauty, with the simple almond blossom or the wild briar-rose.

One of the first functions of ornament is to com-

pensate, correct, or qualify the simplicity or ugliness
of form dictated by necessity. It is a common
mistake to suppose that this is to be done by over-
laying it with enrichment, and hiding it under a
heap of ornament. The simplest and most obvious
lines on which to build a house, the inevitable construction of a machine, the traditional shape of a
piece of furniture, the convenient form of a gas-
pipe—each and all of these may be far from
beautiful; but that is scarcely an argument why
they should be smothered with scrollery. If the
proper form be indeed beyond redemption, there
are only two courses—either to do without it, or
to put up with it as it is. But it is not often so
hopeless as that. In most cases a little consideration will show that some of the objectionable
features may be omitted or supplanted by others
more presentable, and that the ill-effect of some
may be counteracted by decorative features that
in no way interfere with the use, or even with the
character, of the object. It is not quantity of
ornament that tells, but ornament in the right
place; a few cross bands here and there to break
the disproportionate length, parallel stripes to
counteract the appearance of thickness, occasional
rosettes or flowers to withdraw attention from the
less interesting parts of the construction—simple
devices like these are often quite enough to redeem
a form from ugliness.

The defects of the thing to be ornamented are

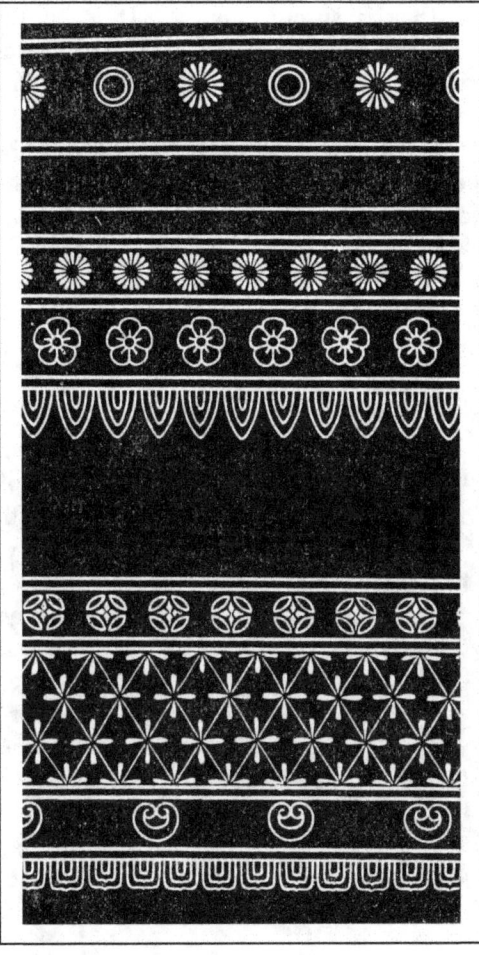

Instance of the use of stripes, &c., referred to on page 74.

the starting point of the decorator. If it be already perfect, that is surely enough. It is because the proportion of a room is defective that we desire to give the appearance of greater height or length to it ; because it is bare that we seek to enrich it ; because it is dull that we desire to enliven it ; because it is glaring that we do our best to subdue it ; because it is cold that we would give warmth to it ; in short, because it is unsatisfactory that we propose to do anything to it at all. The motives that prompt us to undertake the decoration should also by rights suggest the nature and extent of the ornament.

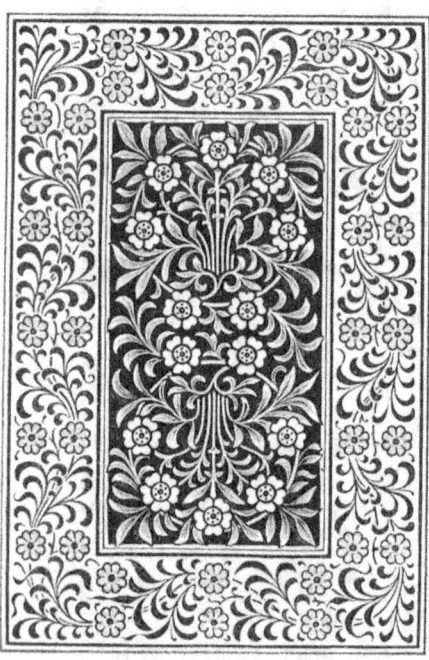

Card-back design.

We could do very well, for example, with perfectly plain card-backs, but for the fact that every speck or scratch on the enamel would be a standing temptation to the unscrupulous. It is convenient, therefore, to cover the back of a card with ornament ; and a design which did not cover the ground would fail of its purpose. It is quite possible to arrive at ornament satisfactory enough in itself but inadequate to the purpose and out of place. It is scarcely necessary to say that however beautiful such work may be, it is bad decoration. Whenever the conditions of ornament are impossible of fulfilment, it is better left alone ; and the conditions proper to ornament are, that it should be fit—for its purpose, for its place, and for the material in which, and the process by which, it is executed.

All decoration, whether of a church, a room, or an object of common use, should have some definite intention in it, and that intention or idea should dominate absolutely, to the least significant detail. Whether the motive be unpretending or ambitious, every stroke of decoration should lead up to it. Every stroke that does not do so is ill done. The first step in design is to determine which shall be the culminating point of the decoration, and however lavishly the artist may distribute enrichment, he reserves for it his crowning effort, making all else converge towards it. Without such emphasis of treatment ornament sinks to the level of dead monotony. The point or points of emphasis being determined, all else is subordinate, background,

to be decorated, if at all, with ornament apt
to a position comparatively unpretending and
subdued.

Portion of an elaborate inlaid cabinet, by B. J. TALBERT,
showing the culmination of the
ornament in panels, &c.

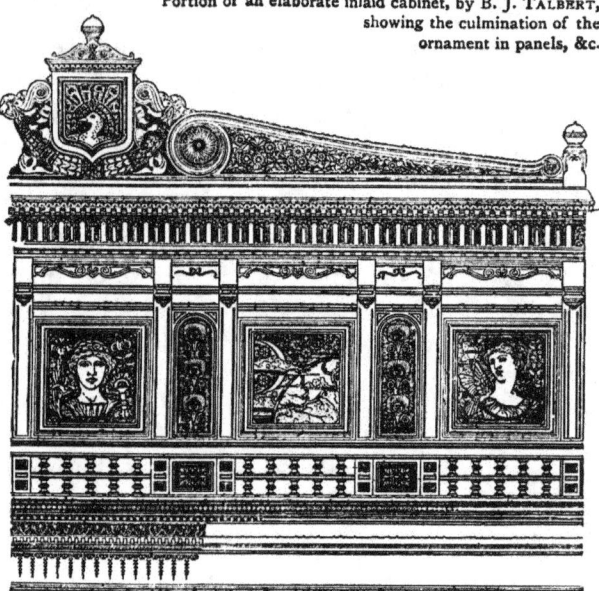

Yet the term "background" is itself only relative.   Walls and floors, for example, are, unmistak-
ably, only backgrounds, from a decorative point of
view, although the enrichment which would befit
the one would be offensive in the other.   It is not
difficult to keep a background in its place, if you are
content with simple monochrome, or with minute
pattern-work in bright tints, that at a little distance

lose themselves in a haze of soft colour, only re-
vealing the design that may be there when you

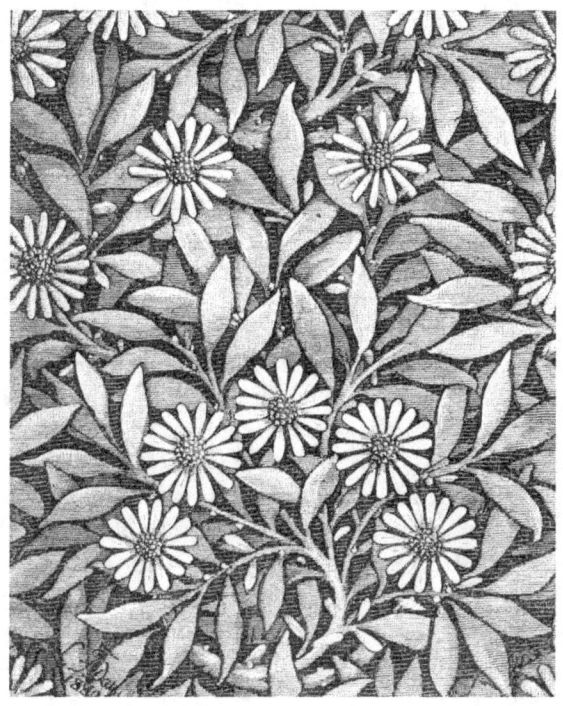

Unpretending wall-paper design.

come closer and look for it. The difficulty is in
inventing a pattern that shall not be insignificant,
nor yet beckon your attention. The unpardonable
sin in ornament, is the attempt to usurp the first

place. It should simply fit its purpose, neither
more nor less. It is equally at fault when it is
too rich or too poor for its position.

We see frequently, set in excellent cabinet work,
panels of so cheap and trivial a character as to cast
suspicion over the whole work. It is hard to believe
that the workmanship has been conscientious and
careful up to that point, and has failed only just
where it should have culminated. Economy is
pleaded in excuse for this paltriness. True economy
would suggest rather that tawdry ornament should
be omitted. The fault of degrading good work to a
position that is unworthy of it is less common.
Yet we do find flower and figure panels, which form
only the background to shelves on which are to
stand objects that will inevitably compete with them.
This is as much to be condemned as uninteresting
diaper or coarse ornament that usurps a prominent
place in a framework of delicate mouldings.

Certain objects, such as things purely ornamental,
and certain portions of objects, such as the doors
and panels of furniture, and the like, deserve prominence ; and in these posts of honour the artist
is justified in a freedom of treatment that elsewhere
would be license.

The panel occupies a position that may be either
insignificant, or of the very highest importance ; and
in the latter case there is little restraint as to the
extent to which elaboration and realisation may be
carried. The law of fitness decrees that it shall

always remain a panel—however admirable in itself, still more admirable as part of the whole. The

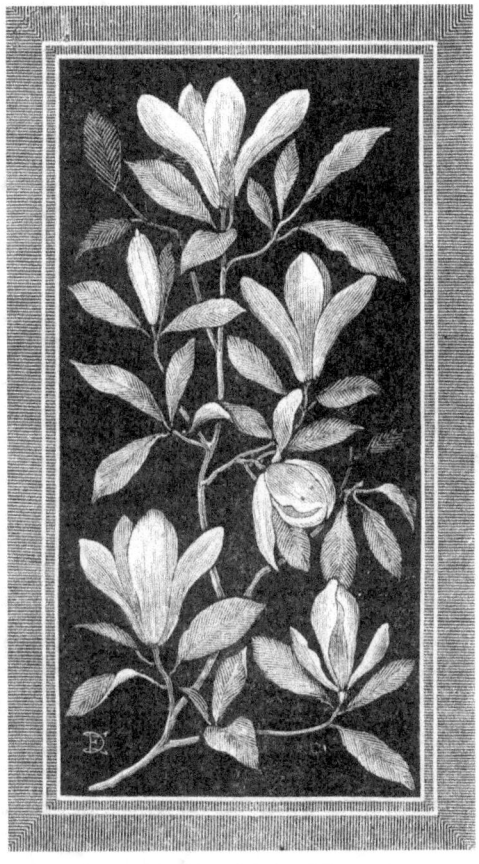

Painted flower-panel designed to occupy a prominent position.

fault of pictorial work as decoration is that it is apt to forget its dependent position, and attract too much attention, either to itself, or to the object

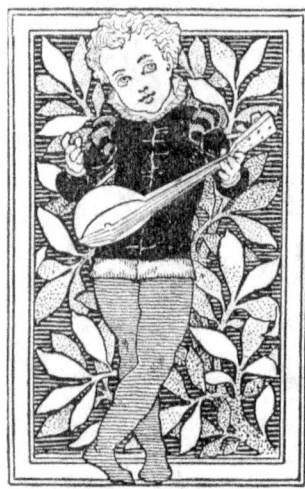

Inlaid cabinet door-panel.

which it pretends to honour. But if it only fulfil this condition of fitness, or decorative unity, for the rest the artist is free to perfect his work to his heart's content ; and it is neither more nor less than pedantry or incompetence that would hinder him from doing his utmost.

There are many ways in which a decorative painting, artistically on a level with the pictures on the walls, may acknowledge that it is part of the wall or cabinet in which it is framed. The evidence that it was designed to occupy the space it fills, its unobtrusive colour, or the fact that it forms as it were a high note of the prevailing tone, may suffice to show that it has no desire whatever to step forward and assert itself at the expense of oneness.

Another question of fitness arises in reference to the position in which a design will be presented to view. It is generally recognised that the pattern of a carpet or any other floor covering should be designed with a view to its effect from all sides— that it should be what is called "all over"; but the Moslem, whose prayer-mat was always placed facing the east, was quite justified in designing it for that one position in which only it was likely to be seen; and we might with equal consistency design a stair-carpet (which is noticed chiefly as we ascend) on the principle of an upward-growing pattern.

In textiles, not only the fabric but the position and purpose of each particular material has to be considered, apart from the manufacture. The sun-flower pattern on page 84 forms the lower border of a curtain; and, even if the flowers be tolerably bright, they only show as a horizontal stripe of colour, not too marked in form when broken by the folds. As a flat decoration, the design would be unendurable. The folds to be taken into consideration in a silk dress are not the same folds that occur in a silk curtain, and the arrangement of horizontal or diagonal bands of ornament, which are so useful in defining the simple folds of a *portière*, are not becoming in a lady's skirt. If a stuff be not meant to fall in folds at all, but to hang flat, that is again another condition.

With regard to the fitness of the form of any object for its purpose, there is not so much room for question. If the consideration of use has been overlooked in its design, we very soon find out its inconvenience. However calmly we may tolerate

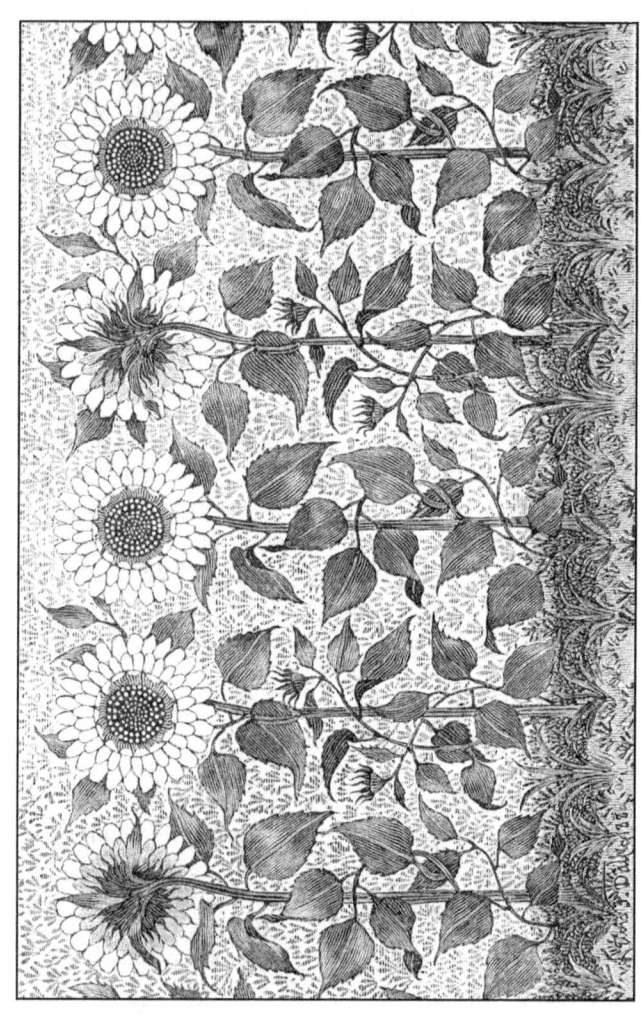

Sun-flower curtain border—designed to be broken by ample folds.

existing inconsistencies, there is in most of us a native preference for what is practical ; and the suitability or unsuitability of a form to its purpose is a thing that can be proved. The fitness of applied ornament is not easily to be defined. Its appreciation depends to some extent upon that very intangible quality called feeling, and to some extent upon knowledge. If a man cannot see the incongruity, that is apparent to others, in ornament which is ill adapted to its purpose, it is difficult to explain it to him. He lacks perhaps the sense of what is becoming, or the necessary knowledge of the subject. There are many to whom the most elaborate and most ambitious work will always appear to be the best. Such men will sum up your objection to work that is finished too minutely for its position, or too delicately for its purpose, by asserting that what you find fault with is that it is "too well done." On the contrary, the contention is that the expenditure of labour which is not justified by the result is ill done. That which is misplaced or out of time is surely done amiss, however thoroughly done. Fitness is essential to well-doing, and what is unfit falls far short of the height at which there would be danger of overstepping the boundary of well-doing, and doing too well. The feeling that there is discrepancy of execution is always an unpleasant one, even where the discrepancy consists in a certain part of the work being carried to a point of finish inconsistent with its surroundings. In admiration of the absolute excellence of the work itself, we may sometimes be inclined to condone the offence against taste ; but, all the same, it is an offence.

Many a time, too, there is a temptation to shrink from the invidious task of fault-finding ; and, rather than say outright that ornament is discordant and tasteless, we wrap up the truth in soft words (pliable if not untrue), and say that it is " too well done."

In one sense only can any part of a work be done too well, namely, as implying that all else is not done well enough—the fault of discrepancy, that is to say, lies in the surrounding work.

The utmost that can be said for the phrase is, that it may be used thus comparatively. In any other sense it is either euphemism or misnomer. Art can in truth no more be too well done than it can be too beautiful. To do unwisely is not to do too well—Shakespeare notwithstanding. Othello did not love too well, but too blindly, too blunderingly, and altogether too stupidly, after the manner of his brutal kind. Much good work is suffocated with false finish, the perpetrator, maybe, justifying the deed to his conscience by the thought that he loves his art too well to exercise restraint upon himself. A far more certain sign of love for art would be in the readiness to make some sacrifice for its sake.

THE WORKMAN AND HIS TOOLS.

"If you do not use the tools they use you."

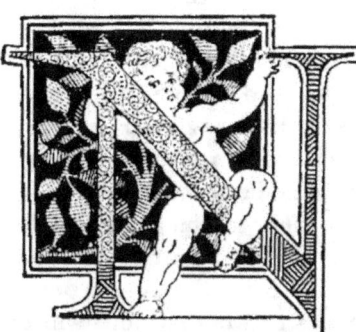

OTHING is more striking to a student of old work than the *traditional* character of the best ornament. Its forms have been handed down from generation to genera-tion, and have in many instances become, notwith-standing their intrinsic beauty, wearisome from perpetual repetition. Such forms are, for the most part, admirably adapted to their purpose, but they were none the less fit before they had been repro-duced *ad nauseam ;* and the fitness has nothing whatever to do with their traditional quality ; excepting this, that it was the fitness that caused them to be preserved ; and that, in passing down from hand to hand, whatever of inappropriateness there may have been in them has been worn away until they are perfect, sometimes so perfect as to have lost much of their interest. The traditional forms and even the traditional methods, however, do not exhaust the possible in ornament ; they are only the prelude to what may yet be done in the way of adapting nature to decorative design.

The distinction between the arts and the trades is at all times rather a fanciful one. The ornamentist bridges, though he be no Colossus, the imagined gulf between them. Sometimes he is himself designer, artificer, and vendor, all in one. In all trades there are traditions, and these traditions embody the accumulated wisdom of many generations. No man would be so wilful as to shut his eyes knowingly to their teaching. The best tools and the best ways of using them may not yet all have been discovered ; but we may be pretty sure that in current modes of workmanship will be found the key to simpler and more perfect processes. A good workman hits upon a new manner, and good workmen following him improve upon his discovery ; and so the traditional ways of working represent the sum of technical experience.

Unhappily, intelligent and earnest workmen do not largely preponderate in any art or trade. Adam Bedes are as exceptional as they are worthy. The lazy find out cheap and easy ways of shirking honest work, and succeeding lazy ones carry these tricks to the furthest possible point. One favourite expedient of laziness is never to go out of the beaten track, never to do anything that is new and exacts thought, but to reproduce the same old well-worn pattern, till a man can do it almost with his eyes shut, certainly without consciously bringing his brains into play ; and his handiwork has about as much feeling in it as if it had been cast in a machine. It has been cast in a machine. And this stereotyped and lifeless detail has come to be called " conventional " ! Laziness, however, is only one of the vices incidental to craftsmanship of whatever kind. " Scamping " cannot quite fairly be identified with "that which has been agreed upon by mutual consent." It would be nearer the truth to say, that not until all possibility of growth has ceased in it, is it possible for an art to crystallise into forms which are altogether conventional. That kind of conventionality which comes of knowing how to use one's tools with effect, controls to some extent the character of all good ornament, but it does not impose the slightest restraint upon variety, invention, or individuality. It will save confusion however if we describe such treatment by a name which does not suggest any other meaning, and simply call it "apt." Clearly art is apt inasmuch as it is distinctly after its kind, embroidery, smith's-work, painting, or whatever it may be.

A workman fairly proficient in any of the applied arts, who is in the habit of thinking over what he is about, *must* produce work that is apt.

If he be a man of any individuality his work will be characteristic of him also, but it will be none the less apt because he has put himself into his work.

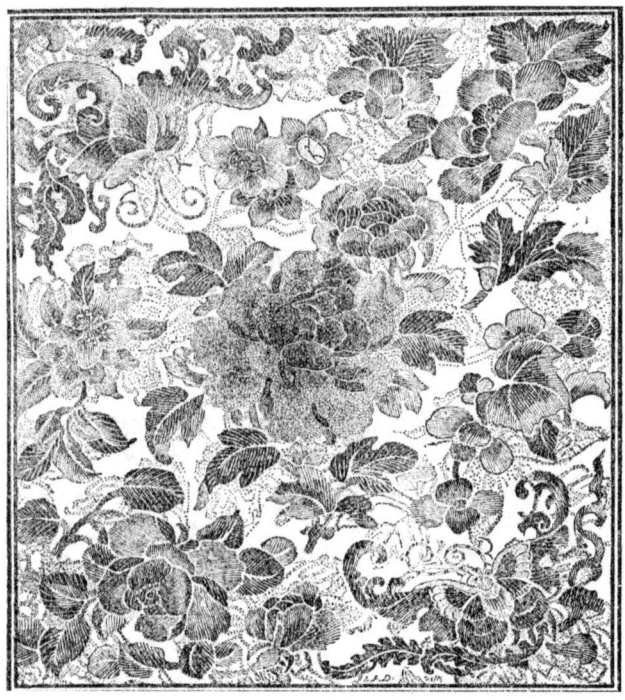

Old Chinese embroidery, obviously designed for needlework.

The least consideration will convince him that, having undertaken to ornament a thing, whatever else he may do, he is bound to make it ornamental.

One cannot properly begin to design ornament until one has some knowledge of what it is to be applied to ; and it is the test of all good ornament that it is applied judiciously, that it does not in the slightest degree interfere with the use of the object decorated, and that it is strictly adapted to the nature of the material in which it is carried out. Misapply the most exquisite workmanship, and it is worse than wasted ; add enrichment that unfits an object for its prime purpose, and it becomes offensive ; work in antagonism to the material employed, and you produce, perhaps, at great pains, an effect far inferior to what you might have gained with ease by an intelligent use of the means at hand.

The considerations of material, process of manu-facture, and method of execution, are of a more or less technical nature, and it would be tedious to discuss them here at too great length. But it is necessary that even the amateur should know something of the value of workmanlikeness in ornament ; and he has only to know it in order to appreciate how unreasonable it is to neglect it. It may require some little training and study, some familiarity at least with the various crafts, to detect at once whether a design is adapted to be wrought or cast, printed or woven, carved or modelled ; whether it is fit to be executed in stone or plaster, silk or paper, wood or metal-work. But it will take only the very slightest thought to convince the least artistic, that the processes of hammering and casting, weaving and printing, modelling and carving are so different; and the nature of hard stone and soft plaster, cross-grained wood and malleable iron, the printer's block and the weaver's cards, are so different, that they demand very different treatment. And more than this, whoever inquires a little more closely into the matter will soon see that each particular material, and each particular process by which it is manipulated, even each particular tool employed in its manipulation, has its own particular limitations as well as its facilities, and that the surest way to success is to bear these in mind, to keep well within the limits prescribed by the circumstances, and to make the most of the advantages peculiar to them.

It is only too possible to work in opposition to natural conditions; and as a boast this may be excused occasionally. Exhibition work is, for example, most of it brag; delicate and reticent art would stand no chance of recognition in the bustle of an international show. In every-day design such boasting is fatal; it leads directly away from modest workmanship and straight to downright waste. In the first place, it is very doubtful whether the conditions will be overcome by the ambitious craftsman—his presumption is very likely to be in excess of his power; and in the second, supposing the result to be satisfactory, it will have been reached by an expenditure of time, energy,

labour, and material, which, wisely directed, would
have gone so much further. It is difficult to speak
in moderate terms of such misdoing. There is no

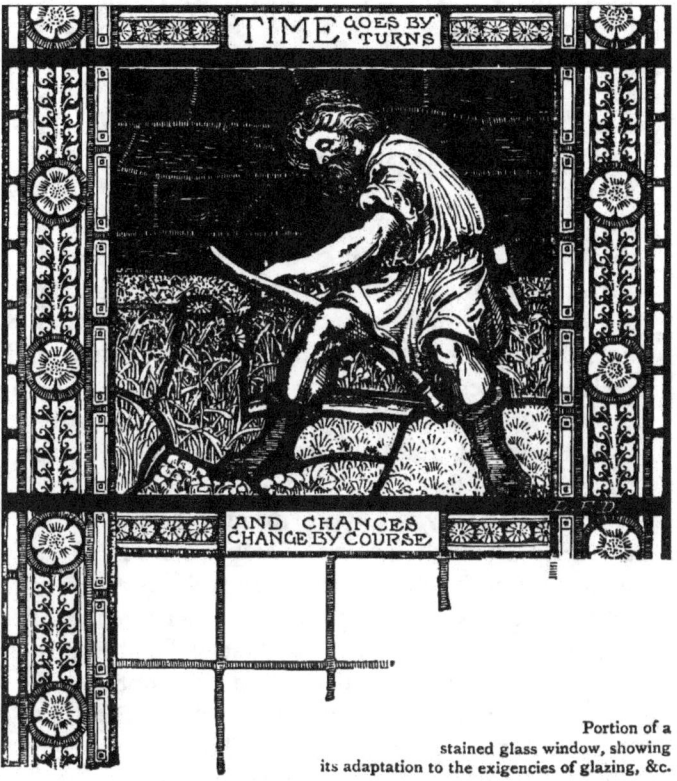

TIME GOES BY TURNS

AND CHANCES CHANGE BY COURSE

Portion of a
stained glass window, showing
its adaptation to the exigencies of glazing, &c.

exaggeration in calling it wrong-headed, unintelli-
gent, unworkmanlike.

Just as the position and purpose of ornament must, it has been said, suggest the design, so also material and method of production must determine something of its character. They need not assert themselves. There is no reason why wood-work should protest that it is joinery, why stained glass should proclaim that it is glazing, or a wall paper shout at you that it is printed. The simple reasonableness of the matter is that they should each be, and be content with being, what they naturally are; and for the simple reason that disobedience to inevitable conditions is, so to speak, resented by them, and leads to labour lost; while to those who work in sympathy with them they unfold resources that the artist had not dreamt of, yielding to gentle persuasion what was not by any means to be forced from them. When workman-like treatment leads to such direct results, the wastefulness of ignoring it is, artistically speaking, criminal. It may not appear to others than artists a matter of much moment whether a material be treated after its kind or contrary to it, but all will admit that it is a consideration whether the cost of decoration be increased or diminished; and it may be worth while to remind them that nothing is more costly than unpractical work, whilst apt treatment minimises expense. Those who begin by encouraging judicious workmanship for more practical reasons, will soon learn to appreciate it for its individuality. It was not until all character had been smoothed out of it by the opposite process that folk became apathetic about every-day art. No wonder that such lifeless stuff ceased to interest them !

The aptness of ornament to material, tools, and mode of workmanship is a virtue that a workman can best appreciate ; yet, in the eagerness to show his skill, he is often led to do just the kind of thing he should not do, in order to show that he can do it. It is unfortunate that the greater number of purchasers and patrons are just those who do not realise this necessity for workmanlike treatment. And as a fact we find that any illogical *tour de force* is infinitely more admired than the most masterly grasp of resource. You have only to put into marble a subject that is worthy of nothing more enduring than a page in *Punch*, and it will attract greater attention than a masterpiece of Greek art. Maybe an enterprising manufacturer will purchase it—for a trade-mark ! Every now and then, some artisan, industrious but uneducated, exhibits an elaborately carved model of Cologne Cathedral, or some equally impossible subject ; and this monument of illspent energy earns higher praise than the best architectural carving would elicit. There was at least one such prodigy exhibited at Paris in the Exhibition of 1878, inviting admiration on the score of the inadequate implements with which it was executed. It is absurd to suppose that a man who has the persistence to plod on for a year, or two, or three, at his self-imposed task, could not have contrived, had he been so minded, to procure the necessary tools for carving his *magnum opus.* And if he could not do that, at least he might have provided himself with the luxury of a hone, or sharpened his knife on the doorstep. To claim our admiration on the plea that the work was done with a *blunt* knife is too much. It is obvious that the industry of the workman was nullified by an almost incredible ignorance. Every man finds his work at times beset, for some inevitable reason, with difficulties ; and if he is a strong man and a bold one he takes pride in succeeding in spite of them. Pluck and energy are manly attributes ; but to put obstacles in our own way that we may have the gratification of surmounting them, is childish.

In speaking of the aptitude of design to execution, it will not be necessary to discriminate particularly between the aptitude to material, to tools, and to method ; the three are so closely connected that the one implies the others. They are all interdependent one upon the other ; and the three together determine, or should determine, the character of ornamental detail.

In the most successful examples of ancient ornament, of whatever time or country, we find that this same aptness is a characteristic ; and one of the main advantages in studying old work is, that we thereby learn how others before us adapted their

design to its conditions and purpose. When we
come to look at the way in which the artists and
craftsmen of past times worked in sympathy with
their materials and means, we soon see that the
limits imposed by decorative necessity are not mere
hindrances; but that they act as safeguards too,
compelling us, almost whether we will or no, to
refinement, breadth, repose, and even grandeur.
Who can say how much of the superiority of old
stained glass to Limoges enamel is due to the
absolute necessity of glazing and the consequent
breadth of style ? If the Greeks had been familiar
with all the secrets of ceramic colouring we might
have had Greek vases as tasteless as the ware of
Della Robbia* or Palissy ! Even the unwelcome
restrictions of economy and commerce have their
value. The necessary repeat of one unit in a design,
as in stencilling, block-printing, casting, weaving,
and the like, tends towards simplicity ; and the
value of such repetition is attested by the fact that
it has come to be commonly adopted for the sake
of its effect, where there is no occasion for its use,
except the scale it gives to the design ; and that is
always valuable in decoration.

From the beginning the apt use of a particular

---

* It is only fair to say that allusion is here made to the coloured
ware of Della Robbia as seen in museums, where the full day-light
is upon it. In the place it was designed to occupy, in the gloom
of an Italian church, the effect is altogether beyond what one could
have conceived possible from such absolutely crude tinting.

material has oftentimes not only served as a whole-
some restraint in design, but has actually suggested
much of the most beautiful ornament. Something
at least of Egyptian dignity is due to the employment of granite ; something of Greek refinement to
the marble used in architecture ; while the peculiar
character of Swiss or Norwegian wood-work is,
perhaps, more obviously carpentry than it is distinctly Norwegian or Swiss. In the more strictly
decorative arts, how much of the beauty of *cloisonné*
or *champlevé* enamel depends upon the network of
gold lines that frames in each separate colour ! yet
the gold outline is as much a condition of manufacture as are the leads in stained glass. Think of the
infinite variety of beautiful geometric pattern-work
that has resulted from the need of simple forms
in mosaic-work and inlay ; and the graceful and
vigorous metal-work that has grown out of the
readiness with which a bar of iron can be hammered
into shape.

It would seem almost as if every success in
decorative art depended to some extent upon
restricting circumstances, and every process of
manufacture were suggestive of some specific beauty
in design. The process of incising suggests its
own simplicity ; niello or damascening invites the
delicate intricacy of detail that we find in Persian
and Indian work ; the style of the beautiful book-
bindings of the sixteenth century results almost
entirely from the method of "tooling" ; the best

forms of early pottery were mainly due to the process of "throwing," and the shape of the potter's
hand had more to do with fashioning them than his
brains ; much of what we most value in Venetian
glass is inseparable from the use of the blow-pipe.

The characteristic of nearly all early ornament is
its directness. The obvious case with which it was
done gives it no little of its charm. We take delight in work that was so evidently a delight to the
workman, and enjoy his "happy thought" almost
as if it had been
our own. Apt
treatment of or-
nament is only
another name
for intelligent
treatment. He
who runs his
head against a
difficulty is not
the man who is
likely to carry
off the honours
of the fight, even
though his skull

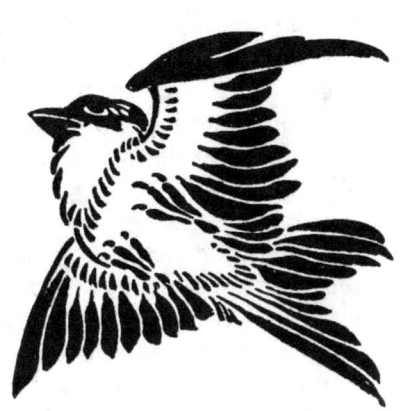

Example of *direct* brush-work.

be thick enough to force its way through. Decorative exigencies are not to be ignored, nor yet
to be bullied. The wisest plan is frankly to
accept the conditions, pay toll to consistency,
and so, instead of making enemies of the means

at hand, win them to your side. They it is that
will help you eventually to the most sure success.
It is sometimes possible by sheer force, and in spite
of everything, to achieve something like success;
but it is always a dangerous and usually a foolish
course to pursue; and even when it is successful,
it was not worth the pursuing. A clear-sighted
artist at once takes in the situation, and, having
realised it, resolves what is best to be done. The
decorator is not yet master of the situation, when
he is acquainted with the use of the thing to be
decorated, its position and purpose. He must
appreciate the nature of his material, in all its
strength and all its weakness; he must be master
of his tools, knowing well what they can do, what
they can best do, and what they cannot hope to do
at all; he must be at home in every process to
be employed.

What a catalogue the common sins against consistency in ornament would make! China is
painted with realistic pictures that have not, and in
the nature of things cannot have, the colours true
to nature, whilst all the beautiful effects proper to
ceramic painting, semi-accidental but wholly decorative, remain unsought. We see stucco bursting
in the attempt to look like stone, when it might
have been so easily enriched by scratching or
incising, or even in *sgraffitto*. Marble is worried
into minute representation of flounces, frills, and
curls of hair, missing all the dignity of sculpture.

Forms are painted in rivalry of the mechanical exactness of manufacture, lacking all the charm of hand-work. This chapter would not hold the illustrations that occur every day, of the way in which we ignorantly or rashly, in any case stupidly, neglect the conspicuous aptitude of a material for characteristically beautiful effects, and stultify ourselves in the attempt to make it do, what in other materials would be easy enough, but what it cannot do. Architecture is to be considered not only as architecture but as stone, brick, timber, iron, concrete, or whatever its construction may be. Lace should not only be lace-like in design, but should leave no doubt as to whether it is " point," " pillow," or " guipure." Joinery and cabinet-work should not only be treated as wood, but as hard or soft wood ; and if the design show that it was either suggested by, or modified according to, the character of the particular wood employed, so much the better. It stands to reason that the tools to be used should influence the design. In simple and straightforward joinery we must be reminded continually of the planks out of which it was framed, of the plane, the lathe, the gouge, or parting-tool, used in finishing it. And though this is not necessary in the more elaborate and costly examples of cabinet-work, at least we ought never to be perplexed as to how an effect was arrived at, still less offended by evidence that the workman went out of his way to ignore the apt and natural treatment of his material; for thereby he proves himself not the more an artist but so much the less a workman.

The conventional forms common to any of the

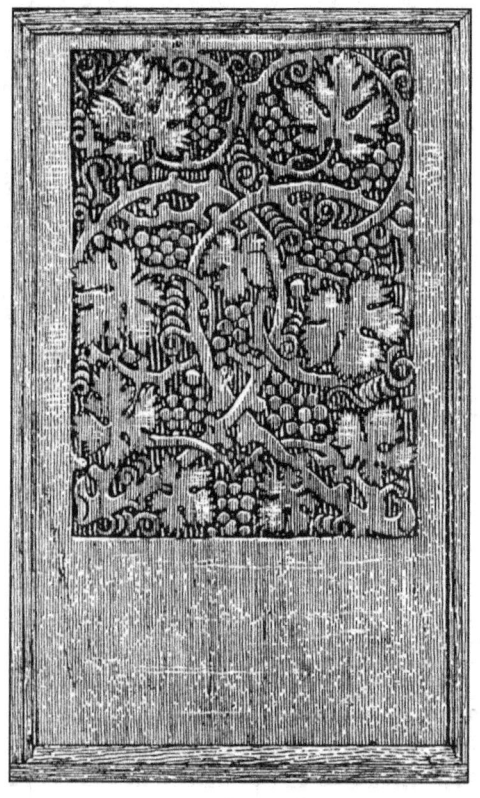

Direct and workmanlike flat carving—Old German.

applied arts are part and parcel of a workmanlike process. If a man who knew absolutely nothing about pottery were set to design a pot upon paper, he would probably imitate to the best of his ability something else ; but if the art of "throwing" were first made clear to him, and he were to begin at once to work at the wheel, he would most likely, as soon as he could achieve anything, produce unawares a replica of some rude Saxon, Roman, or Mexican earthenware. To see a potter at his wheel is to realise how the common forms of pottery could not be different from what they are. Suppose the inexperienced artist were ambitious of adding further ornament, his box of water-colours would, perhaps, betray him into a design intended to rival nature ; but if he had the vessel before him, and the few fit materials for pot-decoration at hand, he would more probably proceed to stamp or scratch on it patterns such as we find on the very earliest ware, or to paint on it something distantly related to the ornament on the Greek vases.

The late Owen Jones suggested that "we are rather tempted to believe that the various forms of the leaves of a Greek flower have been generated by the brush of the painter." He need have had no hesitation in asserting it as a fact. The idea of those forms being founded upon the growth of the honey-suckle is as much a fable as the popular legend concerning the origin of the Corinthian capital.

It is quite possible that some later pot-painter may
have seen a resemblance between the brush forms
he was in the habit of producing and the young
buds of the honeysuckle; (it may as well have
occurred to him as to us ;) and he may then have
exaggerated the likeness in his work ; but the
resemblance to honeysuckle is, in most instances,
of the very faintest. On the other hand it is impossible for any one who has worked with a long-
haired brush, or "*tracer*," to come away from the
vase room of the British Museum without feeling
convinced that the painted ornament is very
emphatically brush-work—that is to say produced,
and in great measure suggested, by the use of
the brush. There could be no better proof of this
than the fact that, though it is so exceedingly
difficult to copy it in any other way, it is so exceedingly easy to reproduce it freely with the
brush ; and that if you proceed to design with a
firm and springing "tracer," you will involuntarily
produce some such forms as are to be found on the
Etruscan vases. And though, no doubt, this would
be due partly to familiarity with the ancient forms,
an unconscious exercise of memory in fact, it cannot
be memory only ; for you will find similar, and
sometimes the same forms, in all the ornament
that has been invented brush in hand. Compare
the Greek work with any other ancient ornamental
painted pottery. Compare it with the detail of the
Early-English glass-painting, and you will find

something more than casual resemblance. The family likeness is unmistakable, and so is the fact that they are all very certainly sprung from the brush. The design below is a nineteenth-century descendant of the same family.

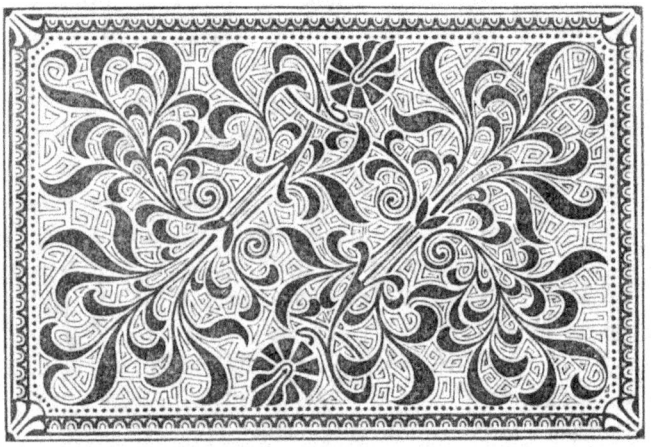

Design suggested by Greek brush-work.

This Greek brush-work is a typical illustration of apt ornament, and deserves to be considered for a moment. The scheme of ornament once determined, we can imagine the painter proceeding, brush in hand, to put in the patterns, inventing or adapting as he went on, and, as he worked for the most part in one pigment only,* producing the

* By the way the habitual use of black is probably only the result of the fact that cobalt on red terra-cotta becomes black in the furnace.

requisite tone by the comparative fullness or open-ness of the pattern. Aiming at no great origin-ality, content to play variations upon the primitive brush patterns, he just put in the design that occurred to him, or that he felt was wanted. He had, no doubt, from the first a general notion of the kind of thing he meant to do ; but he no more knew the exact design he was going to paint than we know beforehand the words our thoughts will take in utterance. His words were so many strokes of the brush.

The spontaneity of this brush-speaking is remark-able. The first natural ejaculation of a long-haired sable brush is the upward stroke A. The delicate gra-dation in its outline is due entirely to the play of the brush, thickening as the pressure is increased, and tapering off again as the stress is relaxed. If you keep your hand in the same position, and proceed to make a succession of these brush flicks (B) they range themselves as a matter of course in the order shown in example C, becoming smaller and smaller as they radiate at a less and less distance from the axis of your wrist. Repeat this process on the other side and you have the

common form of anthemion, D. The other common form, which has more resemblance to the honeysuckle, is produced in a similar manner,

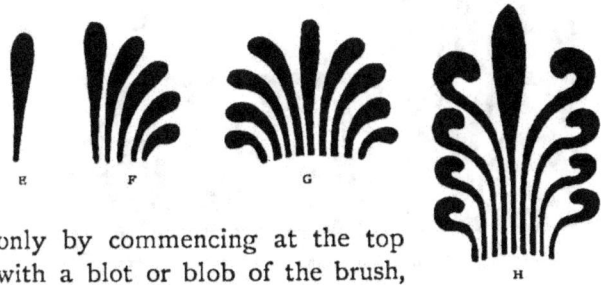

E   F   G

only by commencing at the top with a blot or blob of the brush, which must be full of colour, and gently drawing the brush away to a point below. The examples above show the stroke E, the succession of strokes F, and the com-

H

plete figure G. A less familiar variety of the ornament is shown in H. Sometimes the strokes were less springing and still less honeysuckle - like, as in J. Similar patterns were almost as easily produced by painting - in

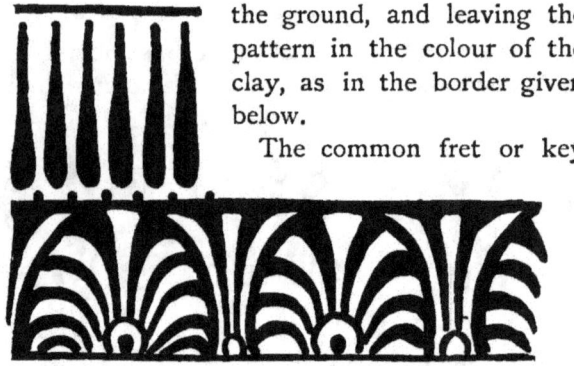

the ground, and leaving the pattern in the colour of the clay, as in the border given below.

The common fret or key

Example of pattern left in the natural colour of the ground.

patterns are equally characteristic of the brush. This may seem not so easily credible to those who are unacquainted with the use of the brush, and who know these patterns only in the printed illustrations of them, where all the character has been eliminated by the lithographer, who has substituted for it a mechanical correctness (?) of his own. If they will refer to the vases in the British Museum, they will see at once that mechanical exactness is the last quality that could be laid to their account. Next to the free brush-flick nothing is so easy to draw with a brush as straight lines of this character. It requires only a blunt brush and a hand firm enough and light enough to maintain always a delicate and even pressure. The difficulty occurs at the angles, and the ancient pot-painters scarcely attempted any great accuracy there. The drawing of a simple fret was done right off in this manner: the

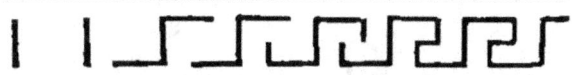

Diagram showing construction of fret pattern.

horizontal bounding lines were drawn first, probably by holding the brush steady and making the vase revolve on a pivot ; the painter then drew a series of upright lines at regular intervals ; from these he drew, at top and bottom, horizontal lines, to right and left respectively ; to each of these were attached again shorter vertical lines, which were finally united by other short horizontal strokes, and the pattern was complete. The accompanying diagram may make this more clear.

With experience the most intricate frets may be sketched in this manner, the eye learning to measure the distances with almost absolute certainty. The Greeks saved themselves much trouble in this respect by habitually interrupting the long horizontal bands by means of rosettes or pateræ, leaving themselves only short lengths to deal with.

The familiar wave scroll may be sketched in two or three different ways. It is as easy to sketch it in *à la grecque* as it is difficult to put it in with the mechanical exactness of modern imitators.

We have instances of ornament which is nothing at all but brush-play. The painter just amused himself by letting the brush go, almost without guidance — and watching the curves that came of it, much as he might have watched the wreaths of smoke curling upwards from his pipe.

Example of brush-play.

The forms first suggested by the use of the brush happened in the end to suggest material forms, and so by degrees some imitation of nature became not uncommon. But for the most part, and until a very late period, the Greeks continued to let the brush control the manner of rendering it. Here is a pattern of which it may be as truly said that it consists of brush strokes arranged in the order of leaflets, as of leaf forms modified by the brush. The bud forms also grew out of the brush. Indeed, few if any of the forms borrowed from

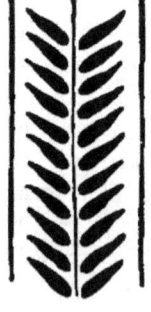

Brush-leaf.

nature appear to have been selected without due reference to the facility with which they could be rendered. It is self-evident that the artists arrived through brush-work at natural form.

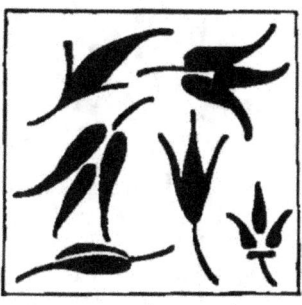

Greek bud-forms.

In this they differed widely from the Japanese, whose art came through nature to much the same conventional conclusion. The character of a great deal of Japanese foliage

Greek.

is the simple result of attempting to render nature as directly as possible with the brush. Working from nature, brush in hand, the Japanese artist almost unconsciously translated his original into the vernacular of china-painting—into brush-work.

It is curious to notice this point at which, contrary to all expectation, Greek art and Japanese for a moment join hands. The Japanese renderings of

the chrysanthemum given over-leaf are as much like honeysuckle as any anthemion, and might pass for Greek almost. There is some similarity also in the Greek and Japanese ren-

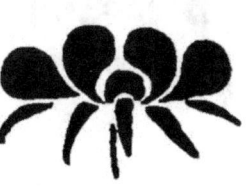

Japanese peony

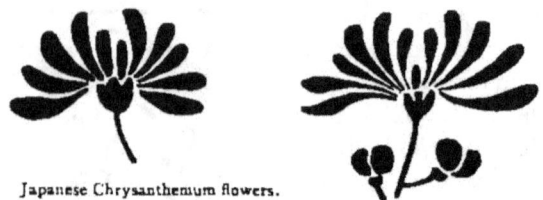

Japanese Chrysanthemum flowers.

dering of the buds; and there is something again in the Japanese bird below, and in that on page 99, that reminds one of Greek brush-work.

It is deeply significant of the connection between all apt workmanship, that artists of two such distinctly different types, working on such different principles, and according to such different traditions, should arrive (the one through brush-work to nature, the other through nature to brush-work) at forms of ornament that may be said to over-

Japanese bird.

lap one another: the apt form seems to be almost inevitable. A fact like this says more than words can say. The accumulated experience of the masters is not to be ignored. Wherever progress has been made, it has always been in the direction to which the old ways led. Design and workmanship have risen to a higher point, not when materials and tools have been despised, but when apter, fitter, more sympathetic treatment has been adopted, when more idiomatic expression has been found.

THE RIGHTS AND WRONGS OF IMITATION.

"Nothing concealed that is done, but all things done to adornment."

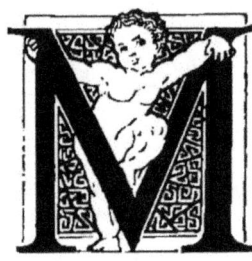

ORE than enough has been said concerning the heresy of shams in decoration, and yet not quite enough. In the many protests that have been made, objection has invariably been founded wholly on moral grounds; and the advocates of honesty have, not seldom, pushed their zeal so far as to hinder the acceptance of their doctrine. Those who do not feel the falsity of a practice are, for the most part, unlikely to be moved by denunciation, even the most eloquent, of their insensibility ; and it must be owned that the reasons that have been urged against pretence have not always been the most reasonable. Rather too much stress has been laid upon the immorality of shams, and not enough on their paltriness. Something remains to be said upon the flimsiness of the device of imitation, upon its futility, upon the lack of feeling and fancy that it implies in the artist who is guilty of it. What pitiable poverty of invention

these shifts betray! What a dearth of the faculty
of design must exist among people whose one
idea of decoration is to make a thing look like
something else! From what depths of poetic imagination can have welled such a happy thought as
that of *graining?* Imagine for a moment the
germination of this great idea in the brain of the
artist, and the logical sequence of his thought :—
" The grain of this wood is not so beautiful as that
of a rarer kind ; but since that is not available,
come, let us *paint* the inferior wood in imitation of
the costlier grain !" Truly a lofty flight of genius !
Yet we in our day have out-soared it, making an
habitual practice of bedaubing a wood which
nature left fairly pleasant to look upon, with a
coarse and hideous caricature of some so-called
" handsomer figure."

Judged on its own merits, apart from its insincerity,
what is there to be said for such imitation ? Once
in a way, as a kind of practical joke, the thing
might be amusing, but no joke was ever so little able
to bear repetition. From the economical point of
view it is contended, and fairly, that it wears better
than plain paint or simple paper, and that the
varnish on it is a protection ; but plain paint and
simple paper are not the only alternatives to pretence, and there is no law against the use of varnish
wherever it may be necessary. An easy, cheap, and
durable substitute for graining would be to *mottle*
the colour of the wood-work something after the

manner of certain Japanese lacquer. This method would lend itself to very rich and varied effects of colour, and, without imitating anything, would wear as well, and be as easily touched up, as graining. Another expedient would be to use for the last coat transparent colour, in several shades, so liquid in consistency that the one ran into the other, producing a variation of tint similar to that which we see and admire in oriental pottery.

The plea that effect is everything, and, so long as you arrive at that, no matter how you reach it, is none the less unscrupulous that the unscrupulousness is exercised in the matter of art. That true artists have used it proves, not that it is good, but that they were fallible. The argument that it pays better to supply the demand for graining, than to endeavour to create a demand for something worthier, is only an argument of the pocket, and does not touch the truth of the matter. There may be no moral harm in this prevaricative kind of ornamentation, but is it not essentially dull and commonplace? It cannot be denied that it is devoid of invention, interest, or character. Whatever of beauty there may be in it, and it is admittedly sometimes satisfactory enough as colour, is more than counterbalanced by its pretentiousness.

A curious fact in connection with graining is that really good work of the sort is almost as expensive as the wood itself would be. But then the polished wood-work would need to be of the best; every crack and every clumsy joint would be exposed to view; whereas painting hides a multitude of sins, and men live in happy ignorance of the yawning gaps in the joinery when they have been stopped with putty and covered over with paint.

Pattern-work, the most elaborate, would scarcely be more costly than the best graining. It is a consolation to know that the craft does not enjoy the favour that it did, and that the "first-class grainer" has often "got no work to do." Nor need we waste our pity on his want of employment; his extremity is our opportunity, and now is the time for us to persuade him to turn his hand to painting of a really ornamental kind.

It is true that many of the so-called imitations are either so ill done, or so misplaced, that they must in fairness be held guiltless of any attempt to cheat. No one is led to suppose that the hall and staircase of the villas in the "Marine Parade" are of Siena marble, or the folding doors of bird's-eye maple; nevertheless the fact that such work invariably imitates something costlier than itself, leaves no room for doubt that it originated in pretence. Evidently the original delinquents had got beyond the stage of copying, like the ancestral apes, just for the love of mimicry; and had learned to delight in costly luxuries, and even, in default of them, in the cheap counterfeit of costliness.

We have grown so accustomed to certain of these simulations that to some people there seems

to be a sort of homeliness about them which they
really like.   It does not follow that all who dwell
in " marble halls " wish to affect palatial splendour.
Many of us who are condemned to dwell in such
places simply cannot help ourselves.   But surely it
would be better for those who have no sympathy
with the pretence implied by all cheap splendour to
refrain from imitating those who have.   Why bear
false witness against ourselves ?   Why wear the
badge of a snobbishness of which we are guiltless ?
If we adopt the habit of pretenders we have no
right to complain that we are mistaken for them :
we accuse ourselves.

   In proportion to the importance of a building,
private or public, is the offence of this simulation.
It is worst where we might reasonably expect
that the doors would be of hard wood and the
columns of marble.   How mean the mock granite
seems on the staircase of the British Museum !
In order to realise all the shabbiness of sham
marble one should see it in process of peeling off
the walls of a wealthy nobleman's mansion.   The
more appropriate the real thing would be, the more
offensive becomes its imitation, for the more obvious
it is that it was meant to deceive.   The quasi-
malachite columns facing a butcher's shop are
comparatively unobjectionable ; there is no fear of
our mistaking them for anything but what they are.
Where there was really intent to deceive, neither
the transparency nor the success of the cheat will

justify it. It is easier to denounce shams than to draw with certainty the line at which pretence begins ; but it is clear that where we have a right to expect a certain thing, and find instead only an imitation of it, the line has been overstepped.

Our objection to the use of an imitation where we have a right to expect the reality, is that we do not like to be deceived ; our objection to it where the real thing would have been out of place, is that the inappropriateness jars upon us. Marbling and graining, for example, must be guilty either of pretentiousness or incongruity. A door grained in imitation of oak stands convicted of pretence, veined to look like marble its inconsistency would be too ridiculous.

In many instances the right and wrong of imitation is not so obvious. The use of veneer has been most indiscriminately condemned ; but it is rather the abuse of it that deserves to be denounced. There can be no occasion to deny ourselves the luxury of rich marble on our walls because we cannot possibly construct them of it throughout. If we could do so it would be a wanton burying of beautiful colour. No sane person would expect the walls of S. Mark's to be built of the precious material with which they are lined. When there is a possibility of misapprehension it would certainly be advisable that the baser stone or brickwork should come to the front occasionally and confess itself. It is a simple thing to embed veneers of marble on a wall in panels (with or without

mosaic work) in such a way that no one could
for a moment mistake it for anything but what it is.

In wood-work the abuse of veneer has been so
shameless, one is almost prejudiced against its use at
all.   Yet it would be a pity that the beauty of rare
wood should be sacrificed to a theory ; and there
is, besides, the real use in veneer, that by crossing
the grain of veneers some danger of shrinkage and
warping is met.   Nothing could be more objectionable than the use of veneer on curved surfaces and
in the framing of cabinet-work, but it would be
arbitrary to deny the legitimacy of veneered panels,
if only the wood be rich enough to deserve cutting
into thin slices.   No one, probably, would be found
to object on principle to veneer in the form of
marquetry.   There is even a charm about the very
frankness with which it confesses its shallowness.
Nothing is left to be found out about it.

Concerning the decorative use of gilding it has
been urged that it must logically be classed among
the shams. And so it must where it is used to simulate
solid gold, as where surface gilding is made to
simulate damascening.   But gilding as it has been
practised in architecture for centuries past, is used
simply as colour is.   In the flowers of the panel
opposite, gold was used merely to emphasise
them.   There is obviously no pretence of anything
else.   A gilt moulding no more pretends to
be of gold than a painted wall pretends to be
of solid pigment.   It neither deceives nor is meant

to deceive. It is confessedly gold leaf. It is at
once a frank and an effective practice, to let the
grain of oak or leather, or the texture of canvas or

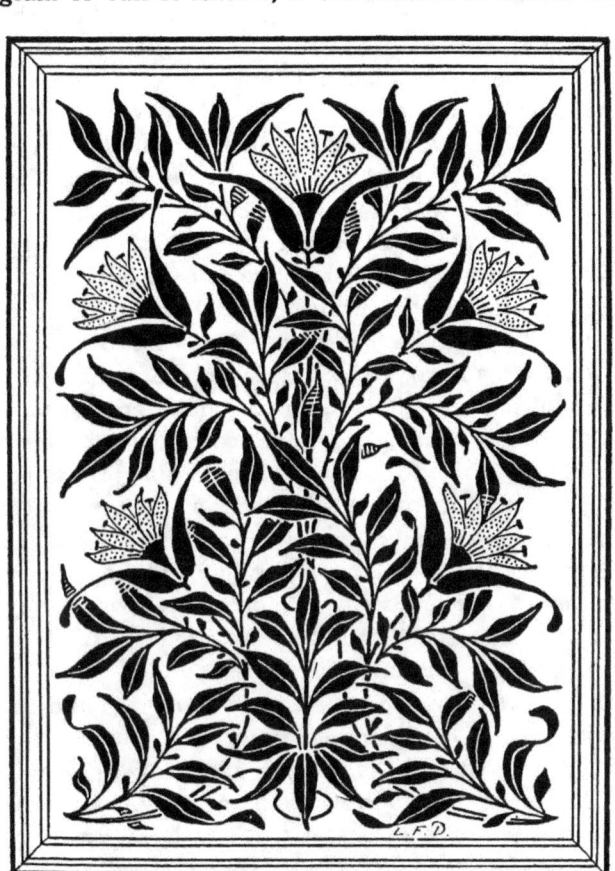

Painted panel relieved with gilding.

plaster reveal itself beneath the gold ; but the
frame-maker prefers to coat everything with a layer
of preparation, which not only destroys all texture
and all crispness of carving, but chips off on the
slightest provocation.

The farce of Pretence is not a new and original
production of our day ; we have only adapted the
old idea to modern circumstances. But the imitation in times past appears to have been of two
kinds, that which directly aimed at deception, and
that which was rather meant to symbolise the thing
it suggested. A familiar instance of the latter treatment occurs in the curtains painted as decoration on
the walls of Gothic buildings. They are so conventionally rendered, and with such obvious disregard
to realism, that they can never have been meant
to do more than suggest the real hangings, which
were one of the earliest devices for furnishing
the walls of a room. The first of these painted
curtains may have merited the praise due to
a "conceit," but the repetition of the freak
ceases to be amusing. Another favourite fancy
of Gothic artists was the so-called "brick" or
"masonry" pattern, a diaper formed on the
lines taken by the mortar joints of a building.
There is a considerable decorative use in the
rigidity of these lines, but the notion of rigidity is
all that we need borrow from masonry. There is
no occasion whatever to adopt the forms and proportions of the stones used in construction.

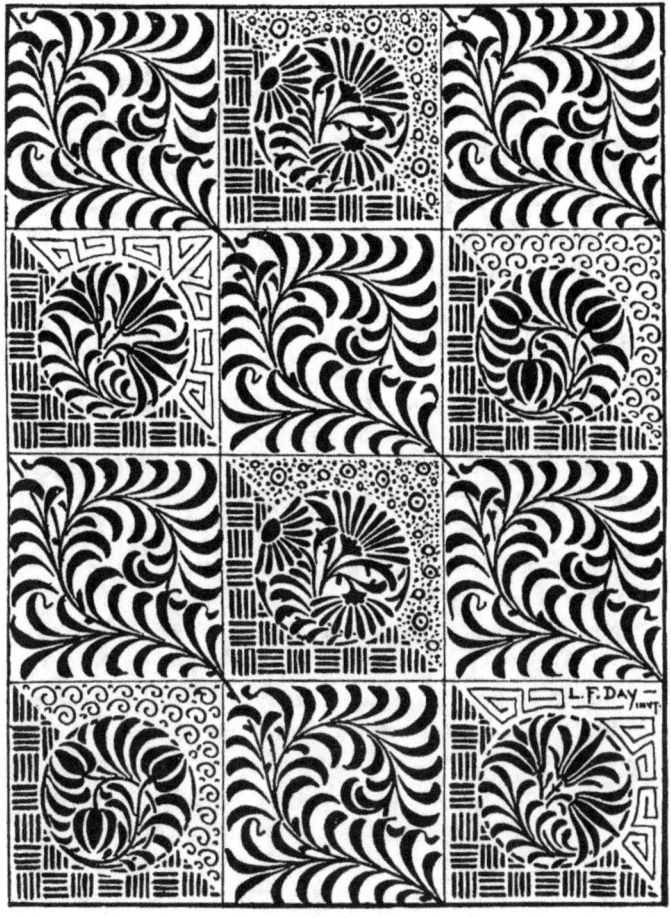

Painted tile pattern.

Apart from any thought of pretence or inconsistency, the poverty of invention betrayed by
the adoption of imitation in place of design, needs
to be insisted upon, even at the risk of tedious
iteration. The obvious appropriateness of tiles for
the walls of a bath-room, and the refreshing effect
of them, has led to the common use of so-called
" tile-papers " by those who cannot or will not afford
the luxury of the real thing. Perhaps it has not
occurred to those who adopt the imitation, in
spite of its pretence, for the sake of the cool effect
of the blue and white, that this effect might just as
well have been produced without resorting to the representation of the jointing of the tiles. A pattern
printed on the white paper ground, or, still better,
stencilled on the white walls, may have much of
the cool and fresh appearance of tile-work ; it may
even with advantage be based on the square form
of the ordinary tiles, so as indefinitely to suggest
them, and thus through association afford additional
satisfaction, without for a moment pretending to
imitate them. The same may be said of other
effects, that have from the first been copied in wall-
paper. The French wall-papers efface themselves
in the endeavour to look like tapestry, brocade,
cretonne, damask,—apparently no matter what, so
long as it is something else than what it is. Yet
the effect might in all cases have been arrived at
without simulation. We may take it that the
imitator knows this well enough, but simply shirks

the difficulty. Numberless are the expedients, more or less pretentious, that are adopted, and in

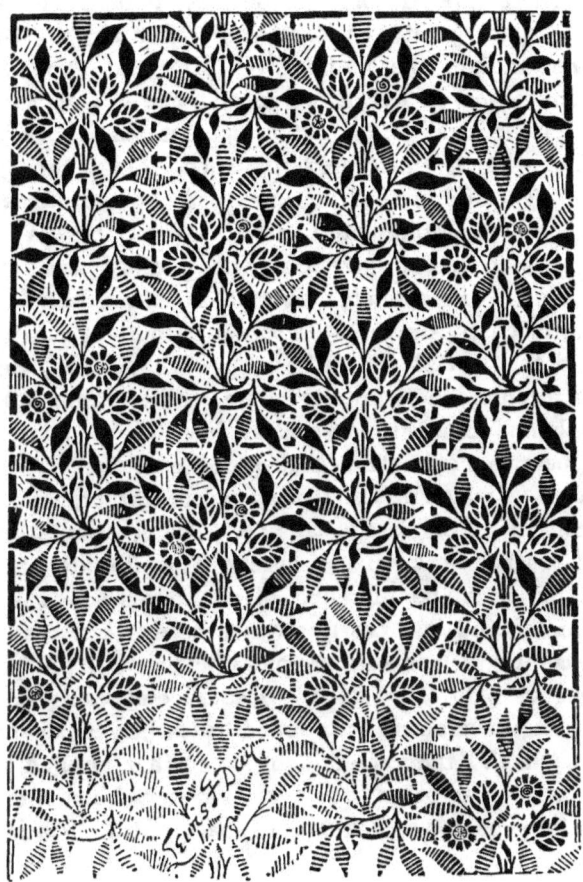

Wall pattern, suggestive of painted tiles.

the name of ornament, to save trouble and supply the place of skill.

There are decorative devices that seem at first sight guilty of pretence, which are not so, even though the name given to them seem to accuse them of deceit. One of these is embossed " leather-paper " for wall decorations. Every-one who is interested in such things, knows the rich effects that in times past were produced by the Venetians and Spaniards by means of embossed leather gorgeous with gilding* and rich colour. These effects have in our time been re-produced by similarly embossing a pulp of paper ; and the so-called "leather-paper" has everything to recommend it but its name, which brands it as a sham. But this is scarcely just. It is not the appearance of leather that is imitated, but rather an effect which was first produced in leather, having really little or no special and peculiar adaptation to leather-work. It is surely a legitimate step towards the popularising of art to reproduce, by simpler and less costly means, the rich but costly decoration which was beyond the reach of all but persons of great wealth. Because embossing and gilding have been first applied to leather, that is no reason why they should not be further applied to paper or any other substance that may be adapted to the process ; and the fact of that prior application

---

* Or, rather, lacquered silver.

of the process does not justify the charge of pretence against those who discover a wider field for its application.

The excuse for frank imitation lies sometimes in its very frankness. The Japanese have a passion for imitation; they delight in it for its own sake apparently, and they imitate anything and everything, reproducing in the costliest material all the character of a commoner substance. They will carve a tusk of ivory into the semblance of a bit of common bamboo—there is at least no suggestion of cheap display in that. Nor is it at all certain that their so-called leather-papers are really meant to imitate gilt leather, though they naturally suggested it to us, who were familiar with nothing of the sort except the old stamped leather. However that may be, the Japanese use paper habitually where we should use leather, linen, or even wood. It would be difficult to say the use to which they have not put paper; and it would seem more just to say that they have developed the resources of paper, than to condemn them of pretence. It is a point not always easy to decide, but certainly worth consideration, how far any rivalry of one material by another may be considered a workman-like development of its capacities, and how far it is mere pretence. Upon the solution of that question depends the justification of the artist. It is to be regretted that our earlier familiarity with embossing as applied to leather should suggest inevitably the

idea of imitation when it comes to be applied to any
other substance. If it were the grain of the leather
that was imitated, then the case would be different.
But there is no such natural connection between
leather and embossing, as to preclude the embossing of any and every other substance that
admits of it. Embossed leather is perhaps in its
origin only an imitation of *repoussé* metal-work ;
and if the art of embossing were traced back to its
beginning, it might prove to be simply a substitute
for carving or modelling.

In connection with the subject of pretence, occurs
the question as to how far one is justified in suggesting in painted decoration the appearance of relief.
The theory of flat decoration for flat surfaces is
logical enough, but it is possible to ride it too hard.
Certainly a surface that ought to look flat, such as
a floor, should not be enriched by the semblance of
objects in relief ; but it does not follow that all
surfaces in which we are accustomed to flatness
must, in the nature of things, be treated flatly ;
though the effect of any marked deviation from the
accustomed treatment would probably not be
pleasing. The walls of our dwelling rooms are flat
for the simple reason that it is the readiest way of
finishing them, the cheapest, the cleanliest, the
easiest on which to hang pictures or aught else.
Any attempt at the appearance of prominent relief
in a wall-pattern would be offensive, not simply on
account of its deceptiveness, but because it would

surely assert itself more than a background should. If, however, not aiming at relief, the designer should arrive at a satisfactory result, which, without shadow or perspective, somehow suggested slight and delicate relief, such as would not be otherwise than pleasing to the eye if it had actually been modelled, it would be dogmatic to declare that such an effect was not legitimate. We have to beware of bigotry. " The truth, the whole truth, and nothing but the truth," is a fiction of the law. Morally it may be desirable ; socially it is impossible. The man who, in season and out of season, is perpetually parading his truthfulness, comes to be put down as a prig. Art, too, may be priggish ; and neither in art nor in life is priggishness an estimable trait. What we do esteem in men and in their work is sincerity, and that is quite possible in the art, as in the life, of every day. The earnest workman puts himself into his work, and if he be frank and honest his art will not belie him by any falsity.

If we speak without prejudice, we must admit that it is very difficult to define the limits of what is allowable. In some cases it is perhaps only the *intention* that determines whether an expedient is right or wrong. A certain degree of downright imitation might not be altogether inexcusable if the motive were merely the laudable desire to bridge over some abrupt transition from ornament in bold relief to flat painted-decoration. If the choice lie only between two evils, one is not to be blamed for choosing the lesser; and incongruity is an evil, just as imitation is: which is the greater of the two may, in exceptional cases, be matter of dispute. In mural decoration one is continually compelled to approach so far at least in the direction of imitation as to give in painting the *value*, if not the effect, of modelling or carving. If every builder were an artist, it would not be so. But every decorator has at times to balance constructed ornament by painted decoration, for which there should have been no occasion. In the attempt to accomplish this he may do something which is in danger of being mistaken for relief, in which case the fault may more justly be debited to the blunderer whose shortcomings he is endeavouring in all honesty to make good. When there is this occasion to balance actual construction by ornament, or where the

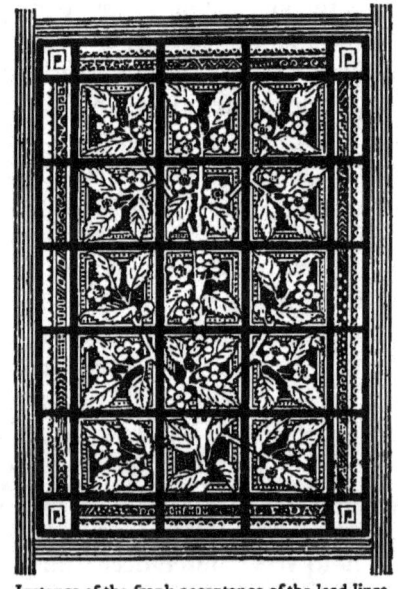

Instance of the frank acceptance of the lead-lines
in window-glazing.

material used in parts of the construction is not carried all through, the too ready resort to imitation is a confession either of incompetence or laziness. The artist who is in earnest will be loth to admit that he can find no mean which is enough for all decorative purposes, and not too much for frankness.

We ask not only for honesty, but for a certain amount of frankness, in the use of a material. The degree to which such honesty and frankness should be carried each one must determine according to his conscience and according to his temperament ; feeling will often anticipate reason in pointing the way that is right. Is it not always so ? The best of us do not inhabit a " Palace of Truth." Upright men, who would scorn deliberately to lie, make daily concessions to social convenience that are not consistent with strict truth. They would vindicate themselves, perhaps, by saying that in their lives they are truthful men, and that it is only the literal truth which they appear to violate. And in art, also, it is not so essential that our work should be true to the letter, as that it should be frank, honest, unpretending, workmanlike, obedient to the spirit of truth.

LEADING-STRINGS.

"The eagle never lost so much time as when he consented to
learn of the crow."

IT MIGHT seem a simple thing to state broadly the principles that govern ornament; and, indeed, it is easy enough for an experienced workman to give some simple working rules that may be of use to the beginner; but these are not to be confounded with "principles," even though they be put forth on authority. The "principles" enunciated by Owen Jones in his 'Grammar of Ornament,' seldom rise above the level of the common-place, and are, strictly speaking, only a description of the lines on which that tasteful artist himself worked, plus certain dogmas deduced from his own practice. Now, the truths that appeal to us are not necessarily the highest nor the only truths, and when we begin to dogmatise we are like to do more harm than good. One may go so

far as to doubt if any good can come of dogmatism.
When once a student has passed that first stage of
art where he has not to ask questions but to do
what he is told and believe what is told him,
whatever laws the teacher may lay down for him
are useful only in proportion to their elasticity.
They must fit emergencies. Rigid dogma is more
likely to hinder than to help the impulse of his
imagination. It is not difficult to lay down general
rules if they are so general as to be of comparatively little practical use. One might safely say,
for example, that ornament may be so schemed as
either to *fill* or to *occupy* the space it is designed
to decorate, instancing the Arabs and the Japanese
as expert each in their own direction. When
however we presume to lay down definite rules
concerning the lines on which all ornament should
be based, we are in imminent danger of becoming
ridiculous. It is one thing to recognise the
value of the lesson conveyed to us in Moresque
art, and another to deduce from it unalterable
principles on which, ever afterwards, ornament
should be designed. Again, it will not be denied
that the Moors made admirable decorative use
of the primary colours qualified with much gold ;
and it is open to us to follow their precedent.
But we are equally free to work on the principles
of Titian, if we so prefer. There is no one road
to success in anything. What we have to do is
to produce good colour, no matter though some
one else have produced fine colour on other prin-

ciples. Certainly no rules of any kind will make
colourists of us. The energetic advocacy of the
use of primary colours in decoration tempts one
to wish it were possible, once for all, to wipe them
from the palette of all but the most expert ; for it
is only the most expert that can safely be trusted
with anything so poisonous as the raw primaries.

The doctrine of the use of primary colours must
needs be supplemented by other doctrines equally
arbitrary. " Colours should never be allowed to impinge upon each other " ; they must occupy certain
set positions ; they must be doled out in certain
" proportions " ! Certainly, if you will take neat
primary tints, you must take also sundry precau-
tions lest those powerful drugs should be too much
for you. But if the primaries are so dangerous
why take such pains to employ them ? A colourist
finds it necessary to hold on to no thread of theory
for safety ; he can do better than any theorist, without it. He delights to disturb the monotony of a
blue surface by touches of green and grey and
purple ; he brightens a red with dashes of orange,
and blurs it in places with brown ; a flat tint he
accepts only as a necessary compromise ; and he
makes use of the primaries, as the physician makes
medicinal use of poisons, knowing that any excess
or indiscretion in their employment may be fatal.

Most of the dogmas as to the proportions in
which the various colours should be used, are based
upon the fact, or fancy, that a ray of sunlight is

made up of coloured rays in those proportions. We were taught in childhood that the seven colours of the rainbow went to make white light ; later, we learnt that there were three primary colours, although there was some doubt among scientists as to what those three were ; we are asked now to believe that there are only two primaries. At all events, Nature (who has on the whole not a bad eye for colour) has very carefully concealed from us the component parts of white light. It is of infinite importance to the astronomer and the chemist to resolve colourless light into its elements ; but the spectroscope is not likely to revolutionise art, or even greatly to help the artist. You may dissect and analyse, but you cannot draw up any formula for the production of fine colour. There is just this fact in connection with the theories of colour proportion, that the eye can bear as a rule more of those colours which preponderate in the spectrum. We can endure, that is to say, more of blue than of yellow ; but any rule as to the ratio in which colours should be used is as impracticable as it is arbitrary. The very test of all good colour is that it is too subtle to be put into words. Only the coarser, cruder tints, that can be quite clearly defined, come within the scope of the theorist. Some trouble might doubtless be spared us, if we could consent to shut our eyes, and swallow obediently some such formula as this :—" Take three parts of yellow pigment, five

of red, and eight of blue ; distribute evenly over a
surface geometrically subdivided into small spaces,
with care that no two colours impinge ; sugar with
orientalism, flavour with conventionality at discretion, and serve up boldly in the form of ornamental
art !" But how is one to arrive at a pure primary
colour ? Our pigments do not approach the purity
of the prism. And how is it to be measured ?
The eye must be judge. Better by far trust to it
altogether, and dispense with the encumbrance of
a theory.

And then the rules concerning the relation of
form to colour ! One obvious use to which colour
may be put is that of emphasising form. But to
insist that the development of form is the one and
only function of colour, is more than rash. Surely
it is permissible to distribute the colour of one's
background so as to emphasise only such forms as
seem to need emphasis. Purity of form needs
certainly no "development" by means of colour ;
it is best appreciated in the absence thereof; and,
on the other hand, full, rich colour can afford to
dispense with some grace in forms that lend themselves to its satisfactory distribution. This is fully
appreciated by painters, who habitually sacrifice
one to the other, according as their aim is form or
colour. Its appreciation by the decorator has
perhaps been hindered by authoritative dogma.
All that can safely be asserted is, that in any
scheme of colour there should be strict relation

between its quality, its quantity, and its situation—
that is to say, its quality will be suggested by the
quantity in which it is used, and the situation in
which it is placed ; its quantity will be regulated by
the lightness or darkness, the brilliancy or depth,

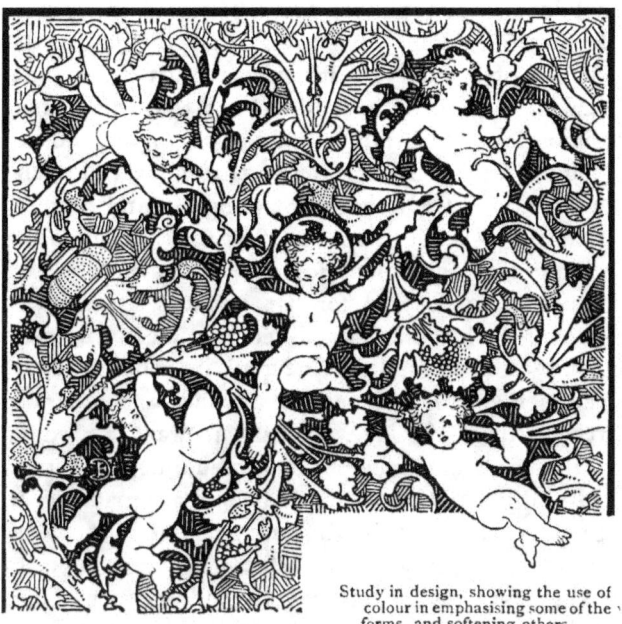

Study in design, showing the use of
colour in emphasising some of the
forms, and softening others.

of the tints employed, and by considerations of
the light or shadow in which they are placed, and
the distance at which they are seen ; its situation
will be determined by the amount of colour used,
and the nature of that colour.

No need of much philosophy to tell us that the cruder a colour the less we must use of it, and the more it should be broken up, and separated from other crude colour ; or to teach us that low tones are lost in dark places, where bright ones are only subdued to due sobriety and softness. The slightest feeling for colour will suggest that the larger the surface of one colour the lower it must be in tone, (unless again it be in shadow,) and that the smaller the surface the brighter it may be. Every house-painter knows by experience that for a ceiling he must mix his tint a shade or two lighter and brighter than he wishes it to appear ; but to insist upon the adoption of one colour for projections, another for hollows, and a third for flat surfaces, is to prove oneself a theorist beyond redemption. One need not even have studied Chevreul in order to know that some colours appear to advance and others to recede from the eye. Where it was desired to throw back one member of a moulding, we should naturally paint it in some colour approaching to greyness, and not bright orange ; but it is by no means necessary in architectural decoration to exaggerate every projection and deepen every hollow, as if the architect had expressed himself so timidly that it was necessary for the decorator to underline his words. When architect and deco-rator are one, he wisely leaves it to the painting to supplement the modelling. He relies, perhaps, upon colour to deepen hollows, as did the Greeks

when they made their curves so flat ; perhaps upon
the depth of the hollow to soften the crudity of
available colours. This is more nearly the function
of colour—to qualify form, defining or subduing it as
need may be. For example, in the grotesque below

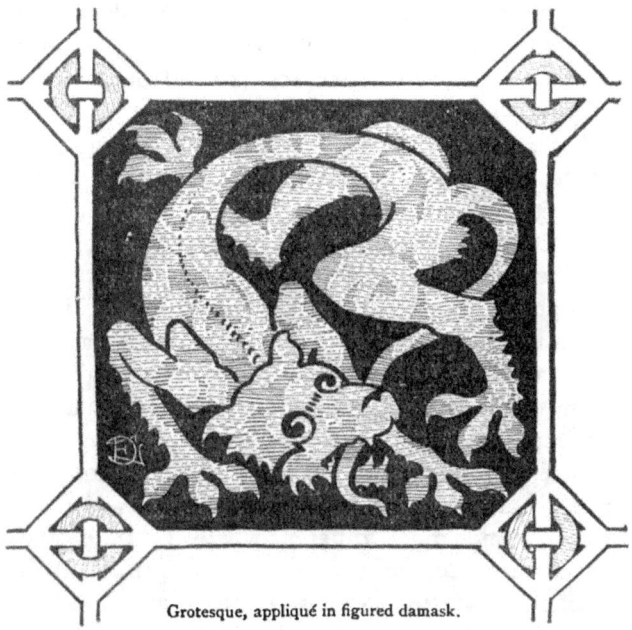

Grotesque, appliqué in figured damask.

the body of the creature is cut out of a piece of
damask, the pattern of which bears no relation to
the beast, in order to get variety, and at the same
time to soften the hardness of the form.

It may even be said that, art being in its nature

experimental, and perfection not often to be obtained, the practical use of colour in architecture (wherein form is of supreme importance) is often to correct and supplement it, to give variety to what is monotonous, emphasis to what is tame, and unity to what would otherwise be disjointed. In many of the plastic arts what is done is done, so far as they are concerned, and no modification is possible. A stroke of the chisel that has gone too far, cannot be recalled; but if the work is to be painted it is the province of the painter to rectify the mistake that, but for him, would be irremediable.

The practical decorator, who has mostly to accept forms as they are and do the best he can with them, would be sorry indeed to have to emphasise by colour what is already only too aggressive. He is grateful to the tones that will enable him to do something towards subduing it.

The relation between the forms and colours he adopts is always in the mind of the artist. If there be not much difference between the shades of colour used, he sees that his forms shall be strong enough to take care of themselves; unless, indeed, it be his deliberate intention that the pattern shall just break the monotony of a flat surface, without itself being obvious. (The pronounced pattern of the curtains illustrated, is calculated not to be altogether lost even in the one-coloured silk terry in which it was produced.)

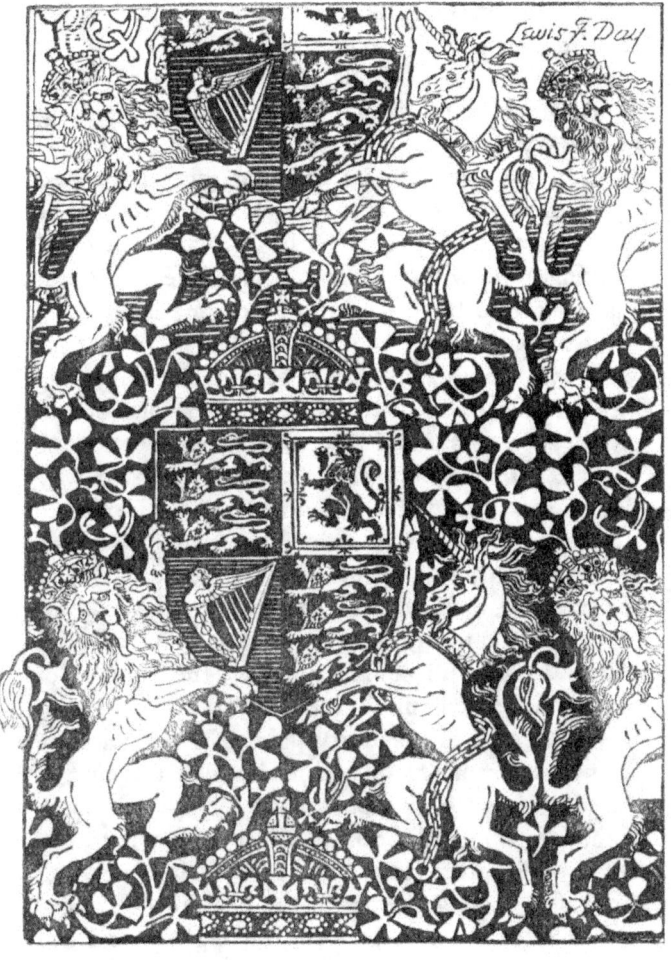

Heraldic curtain design, executed for Windsor Castle.

There are patterns that are meant to be felt by
their influence rather than seen.

Dogma professes to be founded upon the principles of old work, which was inspired by nothing
of the kind. Every instance of good work has
some hint for us ; but its teaching must be tested
by a multitude of examples before we can accept
it as a law even to ourselves. It may be a good
working rule, without being a principle of design
that we are justified in asserting dogmatically.

The analysis of many examples of the best
work will show that in it perfect harmony has
often resulted from the exclusion of one of the
primary colours ; and the timely recollection of
that experience may suggest to the artist a way
out of his immediate difficulty ; but to formulate
that experience into a rule for general guidance,
would be only less pernicious than to insist upon
the presence, always, of all the primaries. We know
very well that any considerable volume of one
colour is kept in countenance by the support of
some kindred colour in the composition, and that
the occurrence of a solitary point of vivid colour is
an invaluable means of emphasis. We feel that in
the decoration of a room there should be some
gradation upwards both of form and colour. It
seems only natural that the deeper colour and the
more rigid form should be at the base of the design,
and that the tones should grow lighter and the
lines freer as they ascend. There is no limit to the

suggestions of experience ; but who shall say that there is one way, and only one, of balancing or emphasising colour ; or that a delightful effect of wall decoration may not be produced without upward gradation of colour, and without any severity of form whatever ?

In the difficulties of design, every hint, however slight, is valuable ; but all dogma is insupportable. The cultivated instinct of the artist must be its own law. Let him dare to be true to his artistic conscience, and he can afford to despise the theorist and all his works.

THE RIVAL CLAIMS OF FORM AND COLOUR.

" No man can serve two masters."

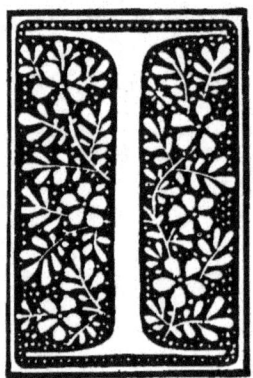

IT is impossible to reconcile all the claims of form and colour. The two work often together to their mutual gain. But, however friendly the rivalry between them, it is always rivalry, and each claims for itself something that the other would fain deny to it. It would seem as if absolute perfection of the one were only to be obtained by some sacrifice of the other ; the dual excellence is seldom found to exist, if ever. There are, and have been in all times, men who in their work aim at combining the two qualities in equal perfection, and who have attained in both a measure of success ; but they are just the men who fail to satisfy, either colourists in the matter of colour, or draughtsmen in the matter of form. And with respect to decorative art, what remains to us of ancient ornament goes to show that the masters of form are often those from whom the secret of colour is hidden, and that colourists are as frequently half contemptuous of form, making use of it merely to assist them in their effect of colour.

Perhaps the very pre-eminence of the Greeks in form was in some measure due to a defective appreciation of the beauty of colour. Mr. Gladstone's theory of the colour-blindness of the ancient Greeks may or may not be correct; but at least it seems certain that Homer did not describe colour with the accuracy, nor yet with the appreciation of its infinite variety, which is a comparatively common characteristic of modern poetry. Too much stress must not be laid upon the verbal painting of colour by a poet, even though that poet be Homer; but it is at least valuable corroborative evidence of the more direct testimony of archaic Greek art. We see in that no vestiges of anything very beautiful or subtle in colour; nor in the work of centuries later, when Greek art was in its prime, does the colour appear to have passed beyond tasteful tinting. Some fragments of their coloured glass vessels are beautiful, but a larger proportion of them are positively unpleasant to the eye. Nothing could well be worse than some of the "marbled" ware, and other sweetstuff-suggesting mixtures, more like to tempt a schoolboy than a colourist. What we are told of the painting of their temples is, at all events, not suggestive of anything like tenderness of tone. In the vases we seem to have evidence that they reached in colour that stage of cultivated taste which characterised them.   As far as it goes it is perfectly satisfactory, but it does not go much beyond monotone. Failing all proof of that full sense of colour which is so common among the nations of the East, we may be allowed to suspect that taste was the highest point to which they attained in this direction, a taste the more perfectly under control because they had no passion for colour.

It is scarcely logical to argue that, because the Greeks were so eminent in many things, they must have been pre-eminent in all.   The fairer inference is that success in one direction was attained by a sincerity of purpose that disregarded all counter-attractions.   Even in the poetry of the Greeks, is it not rather the form that is so admirable? Both evidence and presumption point to the fact that in Greek art perfection of form was not allied with equally splendid colour.   Perhaps it could not have been otherwise, and the perfect purity of form was owing to perfect singleness of aim.

Colour, with its sensuous charm, did something towards blinding the artists of ancient Rome to the value and beauty of pure form.   Though their work may have been, in a sense, a debasement of Greek art, we must admit at least that it was richer.   The purity of Greek art has the air of being slightly cold-blooded ; and one can sympathise with the Romans losing patience with its calm faultlessness, and breaking out into redundant richness.

In the Renaissance the culmination of colour was accompanied by almost equal magnificence of form ; but the latter had not the refinement of the best Greek art ; and, certainly so far as ornament was concerned, the purest form was always in monochrome, carved in wood or marble, or wrought in metal.

The key of colour in the earlier art of Egypt appears to have been pitched higher than in that of Greece, and its success was less uniformly assured. It is true that, though among the Egyptians both form and colour were strictly subordinate to symbolism, in the ornaments which decorate the ancient mummy cases both are usually excellent ; but it is more than probable that the colour was originally much cruder than it is, now that the varnish which preserves it is yellow with age ; and even at its best it is not luxurious. It is always with the dignity and self-restraint of Egyptian ornament, rather than the colour, that we are impressed.

Where colour is indeed superlatively fine, as in the art of China, it reigns alone. The forms employed in Chinese ornament fulfil their intention ; they afford scope for harmony which could not be nearly so readily obtained by the use of shapelier masses ; but in themselves they are usually lacking in grace, and often absolutely hideous. To this day the Chinese when they attempt to copy anything show how little they are draughtsmen. With all their elaboration they cannot give the growth of a plant, or its spirit.

The superiority of the Japanese in this respect is about in proportion to their inferiority in the colour sense. Not but that Japanese colour is often fine; still it is less fine than the Chinese at its best. Also the Japanese have rather an appreciation of what is essential and expressive than of what is graceful in form; they select always those lines which are characteristic in preference to those which are beautiful.

Never was the balance between form and colour held so evenly as in the hands of the Indians, Arabs, Moors, and Persians. The forms in use among them are, without doubt, far less pure than the Greek, and the colour is frequently wanting in what may be called emphasis; but it would be hard to find ornament in which both form and colour are at once so good in themselves and so harmoniously combined as in the Arabesque surface decoration. Neither is sacrificed to the other; we are even left in doubt as to which was the predominating influence in its design.

Gothic art comes more nearly home to us. But with all our reverence for the grandeur of mediæval architecture, it must be confessed that even the most beautiful forms of thirteenth century ornament are rude in comparison with Greek or Renaissance detail, whilst the finest colour of the period was associated with forms the very reverse of beautiful.

The most ardent admirer of Early-English glass-painting will not claim for the stiff-jointed, splay-footed saints of the period any other merit of form than that of embodying fine colour; and any colourist who has studied old glass will acknowledge that many of the most magnificent effects are due, in part at least, to time and accident. The action of the elements has corroded and roughened the surface of the glass, in such a way as to refract the light transmitted through it as no smooth surface could; and the mellowness of old glass is in no small measure due to this. To some extent it is due also to the lichen that encrusts it on the outside, to the monster cobwebs that fall in dusky curtains from the bars of windows out of reach, to the thick setting of accumulated dust and dirt round every lead, from which the colours shine out with jewel-like brilliance, and even to the accident of capricious mending and patching and misplacement of glass by glaziers before the days of "restoration." Admitting all the beauty of old glass we cannot take it as proof of the universal excellence of Gothic colour. The illuminated manuscripts, preserved with a care that is less than kind, tell a different tale, a tale for the most part of a crudity that can only be described as childish. Nor do the remains of mediæval wall-painting give us a very high idea of the power of the artists. Their safety lay in the discreet use of ochre and other simple earths, with which they could not go far wrong.

It is not here the purpose, however, to disparage Gothic or any other colour, but to show that the perfections of form and colour are seldom twin-born. Nowadays, as always, an artist according to his idiosyncrasy, looks upon form as a vehicle for colour, or upon colour as it may influence form. His best chance of success in either is in the subordination of the other to it; and it behoves him to know clearly which it is that he desires to attain, and to give his mind to that, not ignoring the other, nor being content to do work that is in any respect bad, only doing always the best that is compatible with his main purpose. In art also, singleness of aim is essential to success.

The twofold effort may lead the doubly great to a failure that is better than success in any one direction. But the fate of those who would serve two masters was long since foretold.

PART II.

THE ART OF THE FASHION-MONGER.

"Come ; buy, buy, buy ! "

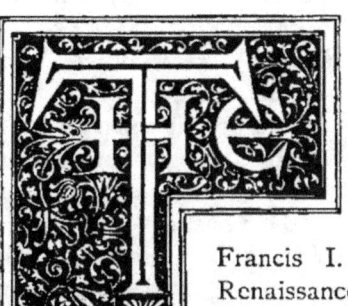

TYRANNY of fashion is no new subject of complaint ; but perhaps it is more a subject of complaint than once it was. When Francis I. set the fashion of Renaissance art in France, no one had much cause to grumble, unless it were the older artists whose art had already crystallised into a shape too solid ever to be made to flow in a new channel, even by the aid of a solvent so powerful as the royal favour. And in later days, so long as kings and queens and great nobles were supreme, and the fashions were really a reflection of their more cultivated taste, it was as it should be. But we have long since changed all that. There may be simple folk yet, who, when they adopt the latest novelty, imagine in their innocence that the fashion was set by a queen or a princess, not knowing how that fashion was, so to speak, "planted" upon Royalty by some cunning fashion-monger. If you wish to make a fashion you must "first catch your" Royal Highness, and then proceed to advertise whatever it may be as "patronised by H.R.H., &c., &c., &c." It is idle to preach against fashion, maybe; but is there any absolute reason why the fashion should be determined for us by persons whose interests are in direct opposition to our own?

Men talk of tailors and upholsterers, milliners and dressmakers, with an amount of contempt which they scarcely deserve; and yet we permit them to foist upon us fashions which not only revolt our better judgment, but are devised with the one idea of diverting our money into their pockets. The very extravagance of the fashions is their device for promoting extravagance in us. The recklessness with which a fashionable dressmaker will cut up old lace or costly brocade, and put the richest material to basest use, is a flagrant proof of the entire carelessness on their part of all but their own immediate interests. Nor is that the worst of it. It is their business to make the fashion so pronounced that by next season it will be markedly old-fashioned, and by this means to stimulate the demand for the newer mode that they will have brought in. It is just the same with the furnisher. He persuaded you yesterday to furnish in a style which he called "Early English," in order that to-day you might be tired of it and try "Queen Anne."

There is a great deal of talk about economy just now ; but it resolves itself, chiefly, into giving as little money as possible for everything. The more proper name for this parsimony would be extravagance. Whoever has had really to economise knows that one secret of thrift is to keep clear of the fashion. The modest garment that is never distinctly in fashion, is never obtrusively out of it. Simple clothes, in keeping with the habits of the wearer, may be worn till they are really worn out ; but the extravagance of last season becomes too ridiculous to be put on when others have abandoned it. That lasts longest which carries no date with it. It is a curious spectacle, that of men and women of all degrees, those even of refinement and culture, submitting blindly to the tyranny of Fashion as if it were Fate ; denying themselves without hesitation that which would give them satisfaction ; and all for the satisfaction of whom ? How meek we are ! How we resign all individual preference and obediently produce our purses at the magic words, "the last new thing, sir," "the latest fashion, madam " !

Fashion is a comedy in which Taste plays quite a small part. So persistently have we followed in the false track that the very sense of what is appropriate, becoming, or beautiful, grows dull. Even vanity succumbs. What art there may be in dress consists, obviously, in the skilful adaptation of costume to the form and features of the wearer, in diverting attention from bodily defect and setting

off beauty to advantage. But Fashion pulls the
wires, and we answer to them. No matter whether
we be short or tall, stout or thin, we wear a great-
coat that reaches down to our heels, if only the
tailor so determine. Ladies wear their hair in
bands or fringes, crimped or padded, all down their
backs or tied up tight in a knot, like the tail of a
cart-horse, always *à la mode*, whatever it may be,
and with little reference to their own particular
style of beauty. Fashion, who crept into the
service of Vanity as her slave, well content to make
herself generally useful, is mistress now, and lords
it over us despotically ; humbly we disfigure ourselves ; without a murmur we distort the solitary
grace or beauty we may possess, and expose our
very deformities at her bidding—and all the while
we talk of taste !

Look at the jewellery we wear. There, if anywhere, is an opportunity for the exercise of refined
and delicate appreciation of what is beautiful, for
in most cases beauty is the only excuse for its
existence. If we cannot afford to wear intrinsically
beautiful trinketry, we can do very well without it.
Not that there is any reason why it should be
costly. The jewellery worn until recently by the
peasant women of Normandy, Norway, Switzerland,
and other European countries (now in imminent
danger of being superseded by the attractions of
more modern, showier, and altogether worthless
Parisian and Viennese manufactures), was strictly

peasant jewellery, the metal chiefly silver, and the stones garnets; but it was good work and well designed, worth transmitting from mother to daughter, and not fit only to be flung aside when the fashion had passed by. Men of discernment have been collecting and buying up the old examples of this work. Will any one be likely to buy up the remains of what is supplanting it? How much of this last will survive at all?

There is this to be said of the better class of modern English goldsmith's work, that a certain honesty characterises it. It suggests "value received." But the value consists chiefly in the weight of the gold and in the bigness and rarity of the stones. This very character shows how little the artistic element of design is considered, or sought after, by those who lead the fashion. The Indian jeweller, according to Sir George Birdwood, thinks nothing of the intrinsic value of the precious stones he employs. He is an artist, and to him the value is in their colour, sheen, effect; he cares as much for them as a painter cares for his pigments, and no more. They are simply a means to his decorative end. The consequence is that he is able to use rich emeralds and rubies as lavishly as if they were enamel; and wherever he wants a point of light, bits of diamond are at hand, commercially of no great price, but artistically as useful as though they were priceless.

Our English jewellery is just the reverse of all

this. We must have fine and flawless stones, worth ever so much money, and masses of solid gold. We manufacture at a ruinous price heavy gold chains, that somehow will suggest fetters gilded; we embed rare stones in thick gold rings or other heavy and shapeless masses of metal, with a sort of idea that because all is plain it must be in good taste; we throw rare diamonds together in a glittering mass, which has none of the charm of colour characterising the gorgeous, but comparatively inexpensive, Eastern work. Art with us appears to decrease in proportion to the increased value of the materials used. The greater the number of diamonds the more inevitably fashion rules that they shall be put together according to the principles that inspire the flaring illuminations which compel attention to the entrances of the London theatres.

Outrageous fashions are to some extent kept alive by the fact that only very rich people can afford to indulge in them; and to follow them, therefore, is the most emphatic way of saying, " I am rich." It is one and the same passion which finds vent among the poorer classes in Brummagem jewellery, and shows itself in rich ones in the display of watch-chains, rings, and necklets, whose whole value and interest consist in the number of rare diamonds and the weight of gold. Diamonds may be a safe investment, easily convertible into cash, a convenient form of settling money

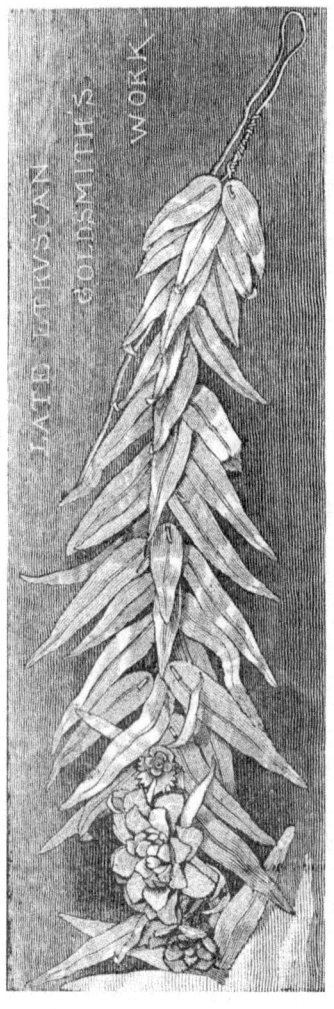

LATE ETRUSCAN GOLDSMITH'S WORK

on one's wife, a ready means of advertising one's wealth—but what has that to do with art or ornament? The Indian craftsman may lay claim to art when he uses stones for their colour's sake. The ancient Greeks and the Etruscans were artists when they beat out their gold so fine that it could be modelled with the fingers and turned to such beautiful purposes as the chaplet given on this page. A crown like that could be worn without oppressing the wearer. Holbein and Cellini proved themselves artists when they gave new value to the precious metals for which they designed. Those, on the other hand, to whom money value is of more account than beauty, can lay no claim to art. The fact that a thousand pounds' worth of diamonds are heaped together without a thousand pennies' worth of art, is in itself conclusive evidence that the wearer does not put on jewels for the sake of ornament.

To blunder in a characteristically British fashion is to blunder nevertheless. We could do with much less of substance in modern jewellery and much more of art. In objects of pure luxury like this, we might well afford to spend more money on the craftsmanship than on the mere material on which that is expended. It would be a safe rule to follow, never to let the value of the material exceed the value of the art in jewellery ; but that would never find favour with the power that is. Such gems would be worth keeping. They would even increase instead of losing in value. Their price would depend on exquisite design and workmanship ; on merit, in fact, and not on any notion of novelty. And that would never do !

If we fully realised what fashion was, and who set it, and for what objects, we should surely be ashamed of following it. Until we are ashamed of it there is little hope of radical improvement in ornamental design. And yet how many of us are there who are not, rather, half ashamed of being out of the fashion ?

If the cultivated will not take the direction of their own affairs into their own hands, but persist in leaving them to the mercies of the vain, the ignorant, and the interested—vanity, ignorance, and the shop, will continue to have it their way, and to elbow taste, economy, and common-sense out of the realms of every-day art.

HOUSE AND HOME.

" That our expenditure and our character are twain, is the vice of
society."

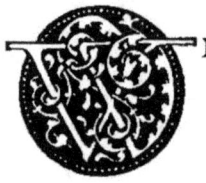E accept, perhaps, too readily,
the Englishman's boast about
his love of home. Few English
homes really look as if anyone
had an intelligent interest in
them. You may go from house to house among
your neighbours, and from no one dwelling shall
you be able to gather a distinct impression of its
owner. Each reflects the others ; or rather they are
all reflections, paler or more pronounced, as the
case may be, of what is, or was, the prevailing
fashion. The rare exceptions to the rule will betray,
not the more loving householder, but the more "ad-
vanced" decorator. If by chance some particle of
the personality of the man whose house it is be
distinguishable, the likelihood is that it strikes a
false note in the general effect. Those who have
heedlessly succumbed to the decorative mania begin,
too late, to find that the little comforts and con-
veniences to which they were accustomed, are out
of keeping with "fine art" furniture, and they
blindly attribute to the fault of art, what is in fact

due to the thoughtlessness with which they adopted
a fashion altogether out of accord with their individual wants and ways. All the railing against
"æsthetic" furniture and its inconvenience, all the
sneers against art that is uppermost in the house,
all the protests in favour of usefulness and cosiness
and comfort (implying unquotable maledictions on
art and its unserviceableness), resolve themselves into
the unconscious confession of ignorance concerning
the relation of art to every-day life. The furniture
that is inconvenient, no matter what the workmanship wasted on it, sins against taste as well as
reason. To revolutionise the houschold is very far
from being the function of art at all. If use, cosiness, and comfort cannot be reconciled with beauty,
blame the artist for his incompetence, but do not
condemn art because he is unequal to the occasion.

It is at the starting-point of decoration that the
most fatal blunders are made. Some effect that
we have seen, some "style" that is in fashion,
something that may be quite contrary to our way
of life, catches our fancy; and we proceed to alter
everything in the house, and, in the name of art, to
render ourselves uncomfortable, dragging that name
into the contempt of all who retain their sober
senses.

How happens it that the word "homely" is
associated with ugliness? A certain simplicity
and sobriety are, rightly enough, in character with
the life of simple, sober people; but nowhere is

beauty out of place. The Puritan protest against luxury, looseness, and extravagance was more earnest than discriminating. The arts, whose highest development was naturally found in princely palaces, fell into disrepute along with their royal patrons; and even yet they have scarcely regained their prestige among the sterner and more matter-of-fact Englishmen, in whom something of the Puritan spirit survives.

Such men will be slow to appreciate the beautiful; but we may appeal with more confidence to the sense of justice in them; and they must needs admit that the abuse of art does not condemn it. Home should indeed be homely, with a homeliness in which ugliness plays no part, unless perchance a man prefer ugliness to beauty. A man's home should seem to have grown round him like a shell; it should fit him as naturally; and there is no reason why it should not be as beautiful as any shell that ever housed mollusc. It does not seem much to ask that our home should appear to belong to us. But the modern manner is to rub down whatever is personal and characteristic to a dead-level of polish, that reflects just what may happen to come in contact with it. To be individual is to be in continual danger of offending against social *convenances*. Thus it comes to pass that persons of real taste fit up their houses tastelessly, intelligent people senselessly, and men and women of refinement satisfy themselves, in this one respect, with something very much like vulgarity.

If we are to accept the evidence of the houses themselves, it all goes to show that, for all the boasting, we do not care for them enough. We are too much accustomed, in these days of locomotion, to look upon our dwellings as mere halting-places between the stages of the journey through life, and to treat them with as little respect as if they were inns or railway stations. Surely there should be some sanctity about our homes. The place where we were born, or began the new married life together, where our children were born, and died perhaps, and where we hope at last to die, has some claim on our reverence. Formerly it was more so ; men were more accustomed to build themselves houses, with the idea that there they cast their lot, there they would live their lives, and after them their son, perhaps, and their son's son after him ; and accordingly they cared for their homes with an affection that men of this generation do not feel, if even they understand. It is not to be supposed that buildings "run up" to let, will ever bear comparison with a house built to live in. The dwelling that a man takes for a term of seven years, in the hope that at the end of that time he will be in the position to remove to a more imposing residence in some more fashionable neighbourhood, cannot excite an interest which it does not so much as pretend to deserve. There is no need to lament the days that

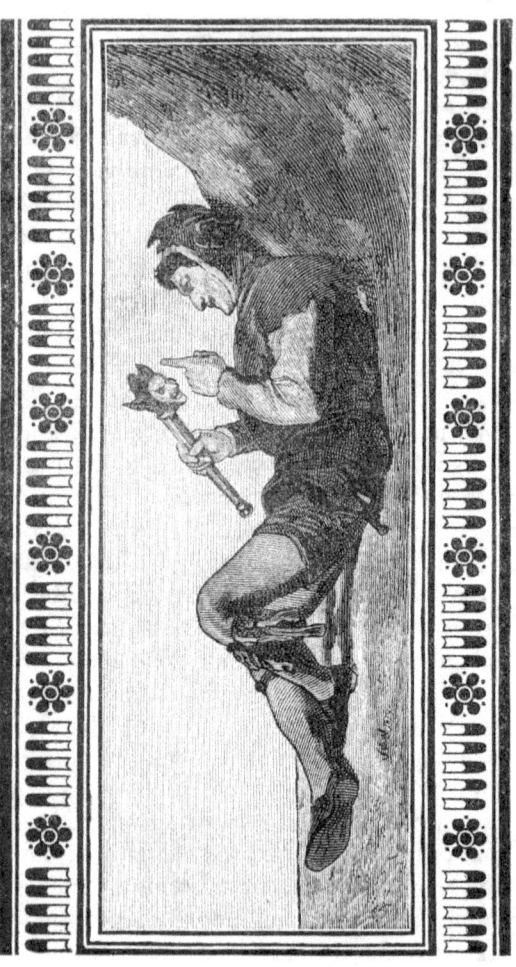

Painted wall-panel.

are gone ; we have little room for doubt that this
nineteenth century is, all in all, better than the
eighteenth, and that the twentieth will be better
still. Nor is it proposed that everyone who has
once taken a house should, then and there, make
up his mind to live and die in it. Too often
it is the case that the sooner he gets out of it the
better. Certain it is, however, that the present
conditions of house-tenure are no more in favour
of the development of art in the house, than is
the restless ambition which characterises the age
we live in.

There is no denying the demoralising effect, so
far as art is concerned, of that foregone determina-
tion not to stay in a place longer than one is
obliged, that eager intention of taking another
house so soon as one can afford it. The wished-for
time may never come ; but the hope of it holds
back the householder from undertaking a multitude
of improvements, both in its appurtenances and in
its appearance, which were well within his means.
It is scarcely worth while to do this or that when
he may so soon be leaving ! He does not see the
advantage of decorating his rooms for the benefit
of the next tenant, or purchasing furniture that
may not fit the future mansion. If he has money
to spend on art he spends it on portable pictures,
and does not commission an artist to paint panels
for him on walls that belong to his landlord. So it
happens that what ought to be done, and under

more settled circumstances would be done, is left
undone, and that which is done is done without
either thought or thoroughness. There is no heart
in it. It has been left to the " decorator." Taste,
feeling, intention, harmony of effect, you shall seek
in vain, but everywhere is evidence of the guiding
spirit of commerce.

The cant of art is just now in fashion, and passes
current everywhere. The business man appreciates
its commercial value, and adopts it accordingly.
There is no necessity, however, for him to provide
art for his customers, when a gloss of pretence
answers all his purpose. It is cheaper, too, than
even the most modest art, and proportionately
more marketable. According to the code of modern
commerce, he is not to be blamed if, seeing that
what his customers want is novelty, he provides it,
nor if, being shrewd enough to see that they prefer
to buy their novelty under the name of art, he
tickets it to their liking.

Even supposing a decorator to be an artist, he is
tradesman as well, and the interests of art and of
trade are not identical. Which way, think you,
will he be likely to lean in his dealings? Of the
few decorators who are artists, only those whose
love of art is stronger than their love, or perhaps
their need, of profit, could be trusted to give un-
biassed judgment in matters of taste. The furnishing upholsterer is, it may be assumed without injustice, neither better nor worse than other men, and

does not pretend (except to his customers) to have
any other motive in carrying on business than the
hope of profit. The curious thing is that the public
should suppose him to have any appreciation of art,
apart from its marketable value. He is just as willing to line your hall with paper that is meant to look
like marble, to make your dining-room dingy, as
well as dirty, by the contrivance called flock-paper,
and to bedizen the walls of the drawing-rooms with
bunches of flaunting flowers that have the impu-
dence to pretend to be natural, as he is to supply the
severest Gothic, the richest Jacobean, or the most
chaste Queen Anne decoration in vogue. What
matters it to the manufacturer or to the retail
dealer, whether the sideboard he sells be constructed on the principles of sound workmanship, or
whether the jambs of the door open with it? It is not
his business to have any theories of right or wrong
taste. Veneer does duty for solid wood-work, and
if the public like it, it does that duty substantially
enough for him. His prejudice is in favour of the
saleable; his preference is for what sells best.
So long as the proportion of outlay to income
remains about the same, it makes little difference
to him what is the popular fancy to be flattered.
But it stands to reason that the risk and trouble
involved in art are infinitely greater than in following any one of the cut-and-dried ideas of decoration ;
and it involves, since most persons are anxious to
keep down their expenditure, a considerable amount

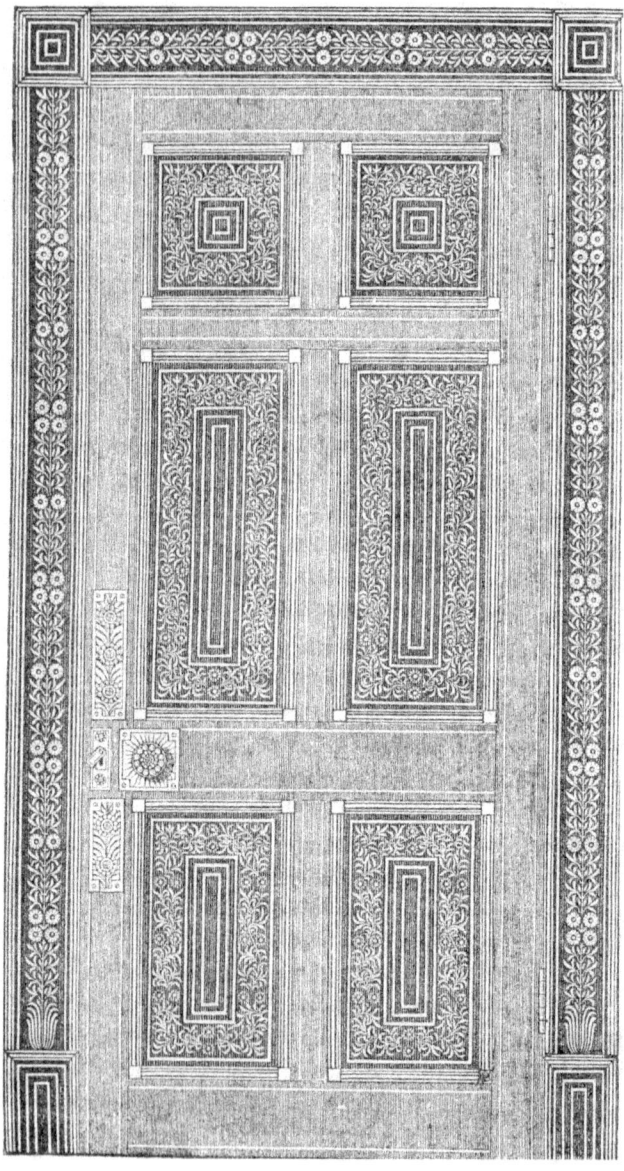

Door decoration.

of added thought and toil and risk, without anything like adequate increase of remuneration.

An illustration or two of this very evident truth will suffice. A room is to be decorated and furnished, and the decorator is called in. He knows very well that paterfamilias has probably settled in his own mind a sum which he purposes to expend, or at all events that there is a limit to which he will confine his outlay ; and the natural instinct of the man of business is to secure such a liberal percentage of that sum, in the form of profit, as conscience may permit. So far as in him lies, therefore, he recommends such things as are safe and bear a distinct and assured profit ; he studiously abstains from suggesting anything that may turn out a failure, or that may be successful only at his pecuniary loss. It might occur to him that such and such a prominent feature in the room deserved special treatment. There is only one door, and that in a most conspicuous position, and for a very few pounds sterling he might decorate it with delicate brush-work ; but the design of such ornament would not be peculiarly remunerative ; there would be some little difficulty in adapting it to the different panels ; and he might not be sure that his painter could execute it with the requisite delicacy and spirit.

Or again a painted frieze of foliage and flowers, after the manner of that illustrated overleaf, might suggest itself ; but it would have to be painted by an artist,

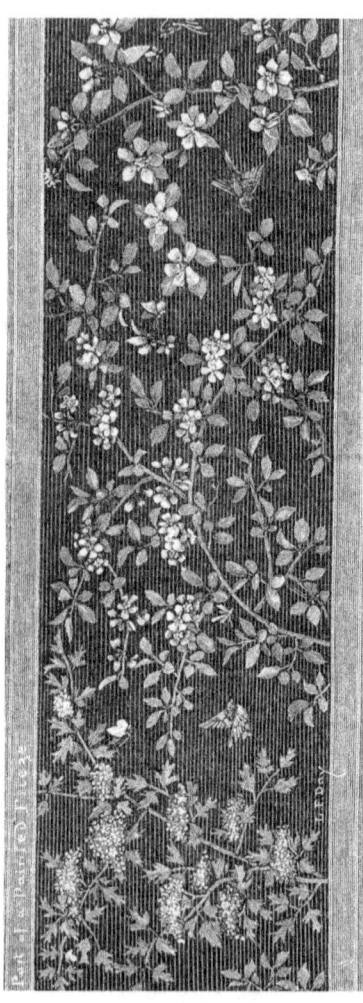

who probably could not say exactly how long it would take him, or what he would charge for the work. So he falls back discreetly upon something more simple, if less interesting. The manufacturers supply him with a variety of patterns of costly papers and stuffs; he shows them to paterfamilias, who is gratified by the "large selection" offered ; and if in the end he is dissatisfied with the effect, no one but himself is to blame, for the choice was his own. In any case, the decorator cannot fare amiss. The material bears a definite profit; the price of hanging, and the like, he can estimate to a fraction; the work is all such as he can depend upon ordinary workmen to carry out and his foreman to superintend; it gives him neither trouble nor anxiety; and the nett profit is assured.

It is no fault in the tradesman that he seeks safety; but the effect of his caution is that we have had to live in white-and-gold drawing-rooms, and maroon flock dining-rooms, to confront ourselves at every turn in huge looking-glasses, to contemplate the "picking-out" of over-elaborate cornices with gaudy tints in lieu of decoration, and to pay for yards of vulgar gilding because that was his idea of richness. The fault is in ourselves. There is no scapegoat that can be made to bear the weight of the universal sins against taste. If small details, which it does not answer the purpose of any but the householder to see after, are neglected, is it not his fault? If we purchase big polished-plate mirrors that we do not want, and ungainly poles which support nothing, have we not ourselves to thank? Whose fault is it that the prefix "drawing-room" is almost a synonym for "flimsy"? Some share of the responsibility for things we encourage must be ours. The "occasional" furniture that is so dangerously light, the settees and sofas padded out of all shape, the scrolly deformity of the console tables, the chairs not to be sat upon by a grown man without danger, were not inevitable. The ribbon-bedizened carpets on which we learn to walk without picking our way, are of our own choosing. Perhaps we are more responsible for the curtains, with their fussy fringe, than for the tawdry cornices that crown them; but the pretence of the fire-irons, not to be used with impunity, is our own; and surely the incongruousness of the chintz pinafores, that cover the covers of cushions apparently far too grand for their place, is very indirectly due to any one but the lady of the house.

It has already been said that the interests of the decorator are not identically those of his patron. The former is able, however, to advance his interests at the latter's expense, and at the expense of art, because, little as he may know of art, of the two he probably knows more; and because, in the end, he does know something of practical work; and the knowledge enables him to throw all manner of difficulties in the way of what may not answer his purpose. The amateur naturally, and wisely, shrinks from the responsibility of that which is discouraged by the practical man, who ought to know best; and so the practical man has it all his own very practical way.

One great difficulty of the private individual is in knowing what is the relative value of this and that. How is he to know that the ceiling might be decorated in simple taste for less than the cost of the tawdry gilding and looking-glass proposed by the upholsterer? Art is worthy of its hire, and decorative art is certainly not too well paid. But neither is it to be had gratis. Artists must live, like others ; and most men's idea of living, in these days, is something more than bread and cheese. None the less

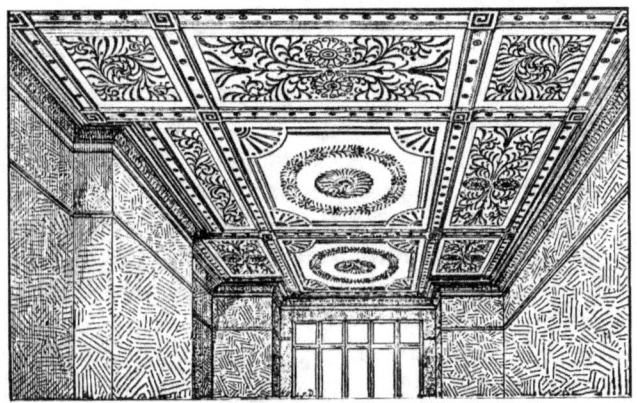

Simple ceiling decoration.

the fact remains that what is paid for, in so-called decoration, is usually not art. Let us say that 500*l.* have been spent on the decoration of a house—it is probable that not 50*l.* of it has been paid for art. Yet all the plain, substantial, necessary work might have been done for 250*l.*, leaving an equal sum available for art.

When the estimate for decoration is sent in it invariably amounts to more than was anticipated. Then comes the question as to how it can be reduced to reasonable proportions. One by one the instances of art, even to the merest border, are eliminated, and the plain, straightforward contract-work remains to be carried out. Much of this was altogether unnecessary, but paterfamilias could not well know that; he accepted what is "always" done for what *must* be done. How was he to judge where expense could be saved, except in the obvious instance of art? That can always be omitted; and so, reluctantly, he lets it go.

Art does indeed cost something, but it is not the costly thing some would have us believe. It is as great a mistake to look upon it as ruinous extravagance as to think it can be had for the asking. The real costliness of decoration and furnishing is in doing what need not be done. Excess, elaboration, lavishness, are what cost most. Let there be no misunderstanding. Thoroughly good workmanship is always the best investment; it not only costs more, but is worth more than the showy manufacture made only to sell; what passes for ornament is very often introduced for the very purpose of concealing the evidence of scamping. In a perfectly plain piece of work a child can tell if the joints be inaccurate, the lines untrue, the surface unfinished. There are no flourishes to hide the faults. It is as if a clumsy penman should attempt to write in plain Roman character; the crookedness of his lines stares us in the face, naked; but, dressed up in flourishes, a very shaky letter will pass muster.

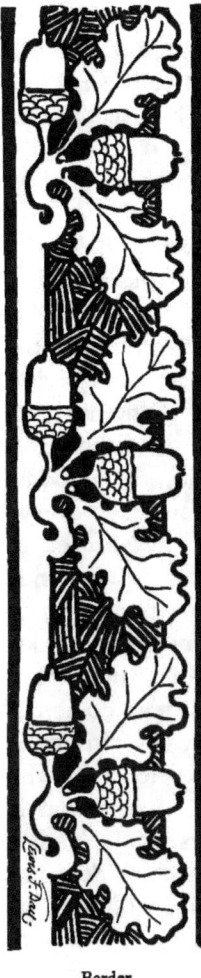

Border.

Thus it happens that the simple, honest work costs rather more than that which is pretentiously florid. Good work minus art is, even commercially, worth more than poor work plus the cheap ornament that covers it; and, intrinsically, one piece of good craftsmanship is worth all the cheap ornament that was ever stuck on to something which was unsaleable without it. The cheapest furniture in the shops is that which is dear at any price. Next to that, for cheapness, comes the plain work which is good of its kind and without any kind of pretence. Then there is elaborate work, more or less worth what is asked for it; but the increased value as art is not at all in proportion to the increase in price, or even in proportion to the labour bestowed upon it. Every exhibition produces numbers of examples that illustrate at once what *can* be done, and what *ought* never to have been attempted in the way of ornament.

Simple work is more likely than elaborate to be worth its price. You seldom find good ornament in connection with flimsy construction. And yet excellence of construction must not be accepted as a guarantee of art.

Too much is left to the decorator ; too much is expected of him.

It happens frequently that the persons who apply to him have formed no notion of what they want in the way of decoration. They should have something more than a notion. It is quite beyond the province of anyone but your intimate friend to divine what may be your ideal of a room. Whether you prefer a light room or a dark one, a rich decoration or a delicate one, is a matter of choice, of temperament, or perhaps of eyesight. If you leave everything in the hands of an artist, he may succeed in producing something very admirable indeed, but which you cannot in the least admire, because it is not in the direction towards which your sympathies tend. If you leave it in the hands of a tradesman, he too, having an artist in his employ, may do something equally good, or something very bad ; in either case, what character there is in it belongs to the particular workshop whence it came. And that is no slight failing in it. The most essential element of interest in domestic decoration is the evidence of the character of the inhabitant. This will perhaps not be very readily conceded ; but it is acknowledged by implication in the common remark that re-decoration gives to a house an air of discomfort. The decoration that does so was from the first ill-advised. What else is to be said of it, when it is not till the novelty begins to wear off that folk dare to be themselves in their rooms, and to admit those familiar and necessary comforts that make home homely? The mistake was in ever thinking to exclude them. The decorator should take those very personal and individual wants into consideration from the first, and, indeed, found his scheme of decoration upon them. He should begin by consulting his employer and finding out what he wants, advising him against that which is impracticable, protesting against that which is tasteless, and striving always, not to carry out some fine ideas of his own, but to put into working order those of the person most concerned. His business is not so much to think for him as to put his thoughts into artistic shape. A mean ambition, you say! Perhaps. And yet the poets are not those who tell us something that is new, but those who most perfectly express for us the thought that was ours before—vague and bodiless hitherto, now and henceforth a definite delight.

Decorative art may quite readily be associated with every fitness and convenience. It is only decorative in as much as it is apt. Instead of detracting from homeliness, oneness, and character, it will add to them, if only we begin from ourselves, if our art be based upon our wants, if our single aim bc honestly to express in our surroundings our best selves. The veritable demons that come between art and homeliness are Insincerity, Half-heartedness, and Brag.

The circumstances under which our houses assume their incongruous appearance, go far to account for it. Before ever the tenant came into possession the walls were hung with paper selected by the builder, in whose eyes those patterns are most beautiful on which the largest trade discount is allowed. The dining-room is dull and heavy ; the drawing-room simperingly pretty. The bed-rooms have been painted with a cold greyish-white, and papered with a view to smartness and without regard to repose. Even if the inmate was in time to have a voice in these things, and chose them with some taste, it is likely they were determined without forethought for the further furnishing of the rooms. Each individual item of decoration was chosen for its intrinsic excellence perhaps, more likely for its cheapness, possibly for no better reason than that it was novel. The carpet owes its selection to the effect of a yard of it seen amongst a distracting variety of patterns, by a purchaser who could have but a faint conception of what its effect *en masse* would be. It bears but the most distant relation to the rest of the furniture, some at least of which was rashly ordered on the ground of its effectiveness in the show-room, and remains ever since a reproach to the discretion of the purchaser. The pictures are such as chanced to catch the fancy of the owner, who did not pause to think how they would look on his walls, or where he should find room for them. The ornaments of bronze, brass, or-molu, ivory, wood, china, terra-cotta, lacquer, or embroidery, are more ill-assorted than all ; being, for the most part, the gifts of various kind friends of very various tastes, each of whom presented what he or she thought pretty. It would be difficult to imagine more unfavourable conditions than these for the introduction of art into the house. It is only after years of a gradual weeding out of the inappropriate, and as gradual introduction of what is really fit, that many a home begins to assume its homely character. Habit and convenience effect at last what it should have been the first object of art to produce—oneness and repose.

How are we to arrive, in our dwellings, at that consistency which is so essential ? Certainly not without thought and earnest effort. The progress of art is no royal procession, but a stern and often painful march. Still it is in the power of most of us to make our home a fit background to our daily life, if only we care to do it. The point is just that we should care ; and if we really do, we shall surely impress upon all about us the stamp of our individuality. Where the builder, the decorator, the upholsterer, the cabinet-maker, the householder, and his kind friends, are pulling each in his own direction, the case is hopeless. Unity can only be secured under the guidance of some one person, and that one should have absolute authority. The proper person would be, of course, the man or woman who is to live in the house. But no one must be allowed to imagine that the responsibility is a light one, or the task easy. It will tax his time, temper, and taste, and he will have often to confess his failure and retrace his steps. Here, as everywhere, experience counts for something. The game is well worth the candle, but it is not an easy one ; and unless you mean to play it out, better not begin. Let us hope that many a man will play it out. In order to do so with success he must first make up his mind what it is that he wants, and then keep that object in view. His wants and ways, and those of his household, must determine the decoration of his house. If all his ambition be a home that shall fit him and his, it need not involve any extraordinary difficulty or extravagance ; but if he cannot find it in his heart to forsake the paths of tradition or of fashion, to break with Pretence and ignore Mrs. Grundy, let him not offend them by a half-hearted desertion, but rather make to himself friends of the mammon of their unrighteousness.

Not till you have made up your mind what you want are you in a position to meet the man whom you may choose to carry out your wishes. Assuming him to be of ordinary intelligence, a couple of hours' conversation with him will, in all likelihood, bring to light the unwelcome fact that some of your ideas are impracticable, or involve expense which you are not prepared to incur. Other ideas will be, perhaps, neither quite out of the question nor ruinously extravagant, but will yet carry with their execution dangers which deserve to be taken into account. In either case your clear purpose, striking against his practical objection, should suffice to elicit some spark that will show the way out of the difficulty—whether it be wiser to retire discreetly, to override the objection, or to try some other path.

It will always resolve itself into a question of give-and-take. There is so much that the lay decorator does not, and cannot, foresee in the carrying out of his notion. For example, it is proposed to decorate some panels with floral decoration, and he sets his heart upon certain flowers for these. Now it is obviously quite the right thing that he should introduce into his scheme those flowers that he himself happens to prefer. But he is probably quite unaware of the difficulties in the way of embodying his preferences in decoration. A decorator chooses from the first the elements of his design with a view to their combination. He, on the contrary, has chosen his flowers entirely from sentimental reasons, and it is probable that their association will involve some loss of unity in the general decorative effect, possible that they will ruin it altogether. Still, if he prefer sentiment to repose, he will very properly insist upon having it; only it is well that he should know from the onset what he

sacrifices to his idea. Many a man has lost the
unity of effect that he really valued, for the sake
of an idea to which he attached infinitely less importance, simply that he did not know how much
his fad would cost in art. He preferred to have the
flowers he liked to those preferred by the decorator ;
but if the objection to any of these had been
pointed out to him at the time, he could readily
have suggested others that were more available.
One may wish to gratify a fancy, without being
prepared to make everything subservient to it.
If, here and there, there should be some distinct
reason, symbolic or other, why some particular
plant is desired, which yet cannot be brought to
range itself in decorative order, it becomes clearly a
question of the relative importance in a man's mind
of the idea and of decoration. Should it be asked
why one plant is less available than another, there
are numberless reasons why one may be fit for a
given purpose and another quite out of character.

To begin with, some are in themselves beautiful,
some not at all so. And of the former some are
ornamental and others ill-adapted to ornament.
Then there is the material to be taken into account.
The beauty of one flower is in its colour, and we
are working, let us say, in ebony or ivory ; of
another in its refinement of form, and we are em-
ploying a heavy and clumsy substance. Certain
forms inevitably lose their character when adapted
to execution in certain materials. Translate the

accompanying strawberry panel into granite, and there will not be much of the strawberry left in it.

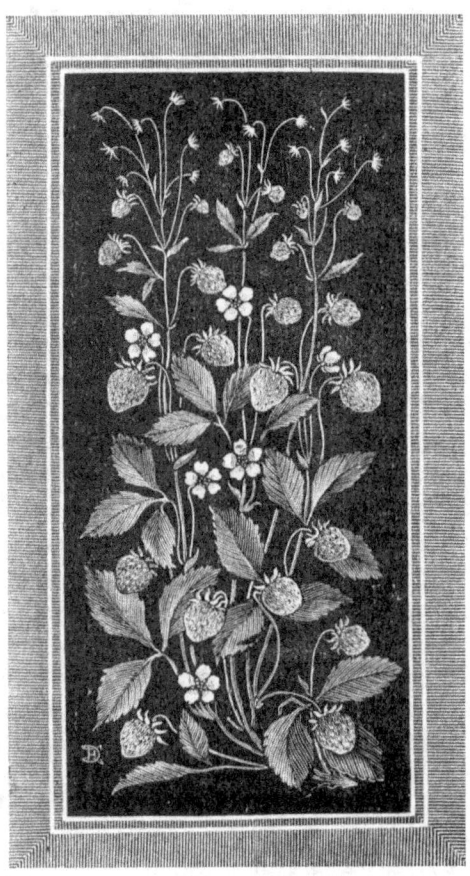

Strawberry panel.

Again, position may determine that boldness is to be desired, or that delicacy is essential, and of course only the bold or delicate flowers, as the case may be, are appropriate. Further, the relation of the various forms one to another is to be considered. Suppose three panels, each ornamented with the design of a flowering shrub, a lily for the fourth would look rather foolish. The relative scale of the various flowers is also of importance. The sunflower is superbly ornamental, but if you determine upon that for one, you restrict your choice with regard to companion panels. Other difficulties occur with regard to colour. Three or four delicately tinted flowers seem to insist that the rest shall be in the same key ; a vivid blossom among them has an air of impertinence. All may be rich, or all tender, or the two qualities may be balanced ; but a series of flowers chosen without regard to decorative treatment will, very probably, be exceedingly difficult to combine into a decorative whole.

It will be seen that in such a simple matter as the choice of flower forms, there is more to be considered than is thought of in the philosophy of the inexpert. Similar difficulties crop up continually, none of them insuperable, but most of them stubborn. Do not flatter yourself that you will not have to give way at all ; but see that you know the reason why you yield. If you do that, the result of mutual compromise between yourself and the practical man will probably be a balance in

favour of your own fancy—more or less, according
to the reasonableness of your original idea.

One more word of caution.   If you feel yourself
incompetent to control the work, or if you are too
much engaged, too uncertain, or too lazy, make one
first effort to find the man whose work you like, and
who may be expected therefore to be able to satisfy
you again ; instruct him fully, tell him your pet
ideas, as you would confide your symptoms to your
physician, and then trust him.   He can anticipate
the effect of what he is about much better than you
can.   It may very likely not turn out all that you
could desire, but if you meddle with him continually
it will certainly be a failure.   " Children and fools
should never see things till they are finished," said
a great painter—a truth none the less true that it is
untrimmed.   We may none of us be fools, but the
wisest of us must pass through that phase of art
which is most simply described as babyhood.

HOW TO DECORATE A ROOM.

"Modern instances."

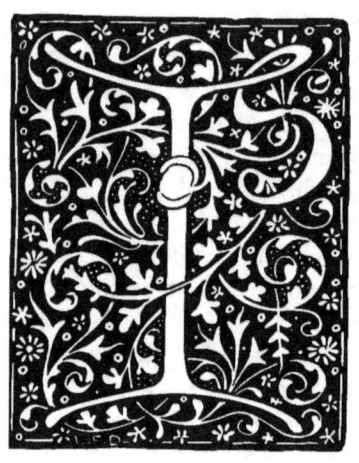

IT because our houses are what they are that we take so little hearty interest in domestic art? Or is it owing to our apathy that they have become what they are? Much of the interest taken in every-day art is assumed. As a fashion it appeals to many, but few have any more serious thought of it; witness the dead level of monotony to which it subsides after each high tide of fashion. It may be contended that whatever is universal must be convenient; and no doubt it is, or was once upon a time, convenient to some persons, else it had never come into existence. But for many years past the prevailing modes of decoration have been consistent in this—that they were invariably ill-adapted to the wants of a large majority of those who submitted to them. It would seem there is great satisfaction to the mind of man, and especially woman, in being as others are ; and to many persons that may atone for everything. Unless, however, conformity be the limit of our desire, the fit decoration or furnishing of a house involves a perpetual balancing of our own real wants against the supposed exigencies of other folk.

Young people of moderate means do only what is wise in taking a house somewhat larger than immediate wants demand, but they are ill-advised in stocking it with superfluous furniture. It is not " the thing," however, to leave one floor of a house unfurnished. The mothers do not quite approve of that unorthodox proceeding. The newly-married, therefore, either take too small a house, which they presently outgrow and leave, or lay out money they can ill afford on objects that they do not want. It is not easy to say which of these two extravagances is the more reckless.

Then as to the way in which rooms are furnished. " Dining - room, drawing - room, breakfast - room, library, bed-room and dressing-room, spare-room," and so on, seem to be in the nature of things ordained, without regard to mere individuals. Man must eat, and he will find it convenient to eat within doors ; but it is conceivable that here and there someone may not find it the most convenient thing for him to set apart one room, out of a limited number, for the sole purpose of eating. Nor, if he do, need he quite see any peculiar advantage in consuming his breakfast in one room and his dinner in another. Again, there is no doubt that it is pleasant, even in the smallest household, to have a room where a friend can be comfortably housed for the night; but the conventional " spare-room " is more often dedicated to pretence than friendship.

It is in the drawing-room, however, that we make the hugest sacrifices to the least purpose. It has all been nicely settled for us (and to question the wisdom of that beneficent arrangement betokens discontent, presumption, radicalism, and whatever else is most wicked in young people) that a drawing-room we must have, no matter whether we be in the habit of withdrawing or not. Inexorable logic determines that because A and B, who nightly entertain their numerous guests, find it fitting to feast in one room and flirt in another, therefore C, who neither feasts nor flirts, should set apart a room for each; and again, that because big A and big B dress themselves in gay or elegant attire, and choose accordingly a light and delicate decoration for their drawing-rooms, therefore little c, whose change of costume consists in the putting on of a loose coat, must also provide himself with a room of state, which is only a costly incumbrance to him. We are all of us only too familiar with those rooms, suggestive, not of the gaiety, festivity, and frivolity of their anti-types, but of chilling conventionality. There is even a certain conventional fitness in the pinafores in which the furniture is carefully covered up; though they do remind one, somehow, of the little girls one meets in back streets, on their way home with the beer-jug, and who seem to live in a chronic state of curl-papers.

A library is, for the most part, a luxury. To certain literary and other persons it is indispensable; it is to them, in fact, just what the office is to the man of business, or the workshop to the artisan. Such a library may be trusted to take care of its own fitness; a workshop *must* be convenient. But the library, so called, might as well have been devised expressly to hinder reading. It is, for some hidden reason, so dingy and comfortless that one rarely sits in it. Yet the books have a way of gravitating towards that centre; and so it happens that when we would take up a book, none is at hand; the dining-room or breakfast-room (in which we practically *live*) "is not the place for books," and in the drawing-room, though there are books indeed, and in very gorgeous bindings too, they are not such as to encourage study. Eventually we submit to what is, and confine our reading to the newspaper, or doze after dinner.

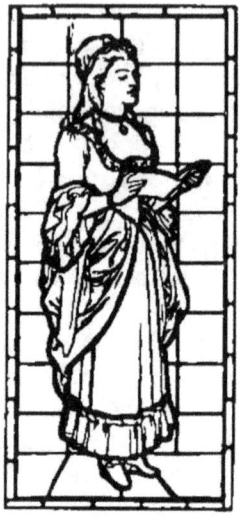

Music-room window.

The music-room is a recognised institution only in mansions of a certain size ; in houses of more moderate dimensions the piano is placed in the drawing-room, no matter whether you inhabit it or not. If you want music by day, you must seek it in the uncongenial atmosphere of a room that, by sunlight, is as much out of time as evening dress before noon; or you must do without it. There is no room in the house for the hobby of its occupant. Much as he may love old mezzotints or etchings, he must put them away privily in portfolios, and on his walls hang line engravings or the sham " old masters " he has inherited, and in which he takes no interest. If he happen to have good watercolours, the drawing - room contains them, though it

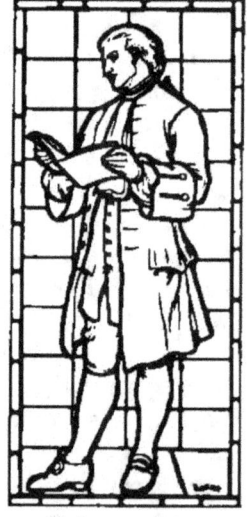

Music-room window.

may contain nothing else that appeals to his sympathies.

Now it is quite true that a room should be decorated after its kind; but that is no reason why all rooms used for a like purpose should be decorated alike. Indeed, so different may their treatment be, so different should it be, that any rules which can be laid down concerning it must be of the most general kind. Take the hall and staircase. There are certain conditions natural to them, which determine something as to their decoration. The appearance of a hall should be friendly and suggestive of welcome. At the same time it should not boast. It should be a sample of what is to be expected in the house, and a fair sample; the bulk should come up to it. As much as possible it should prepare one for the effect of the rooms, and lead to that effect. Further, since no one lives in the hall, one may be permitted, in its decoration, to indulge in effects that would be too startling for a room. It need not be so sober nor so serious as most decoration should be. It may even be allowed to laugh without offence; though the perpetual grin on the face of a living-room would be intolerable. When we come to more minute particulars we find that what suits one hall is not adapted to another. One is ample, another narrow; one is to all intents and purposes a comfortable waiting-room, another simply serves the purpose of a passage. Obviously the attention that the one demands would be wasted on the other. In the same way the staircase, though all that belongs to it may be ruder, bolder, and more pronounced than we should care to have before our eyes for hours

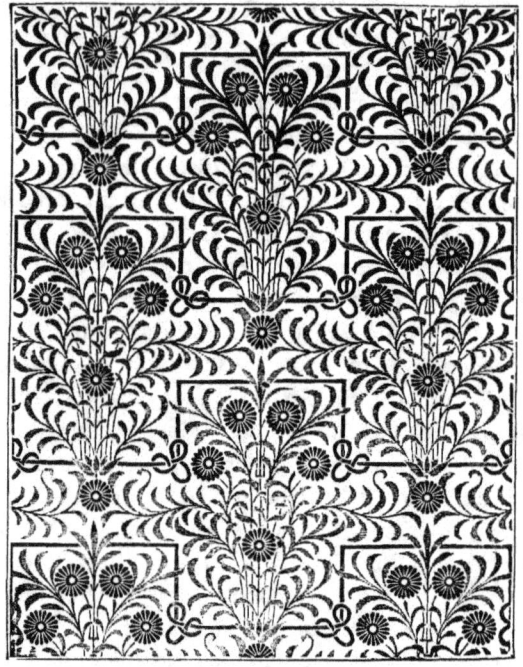

Hall and staircase paper.

and days together, must be considered with regard to the claims of the architecture. The slightly severe but unpretending patterns on this and the opposite pages were designed as wall-papers for the hall and staircase of a house of moderate dimensions, where a few years ago marble-paper would certainly have been used. The mean entrance-halls and staircases usually to be found now-a-days, even in houses of some pretensions,

will not bear much decoration. Ornament only calls attention to their miserable proportions.

It is possible, however, to mitigate the ugliness of the common type of hall and staircase, represented in the diagram overleaf much as the builder left it. The dreary breadth of ill-considered wall and ceiling space, the well scooped out of the stairs, the

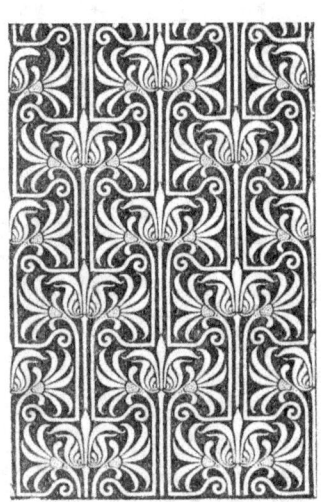

Dado paper for a hall.

abrupt conclusion of the cornice where difficulty begins to occur—all these are more than depressing. The design on page 195 goes to show how, with little decoration, something of this may be spared us. A horizontal division of the wall space disturbs its monotony, and affords a satisfactory line for the eye to rest upon, as do also the bands by which the ceiling and soffits of stairs are broken up into panels. The wood-work which is inoffensive in character is proportionally pronounced in colour; and, in the same way, the panes of glass introduced into the door facing the passage, are meant to draw attention from the graceless curve of the ceiling above, and its awkward junction with the side wall.

With regard to rooms the vital question is, not what they are called, but what purpose they serve. The dining-room—is it a dining-room really? or is it a living-room in which also dinner is served? In the one case, only such furniture as dining necessitates should be there; the sideboard should serve the purpose of a sideboard, not of a cabinet for "curios"; the effect should be considered from

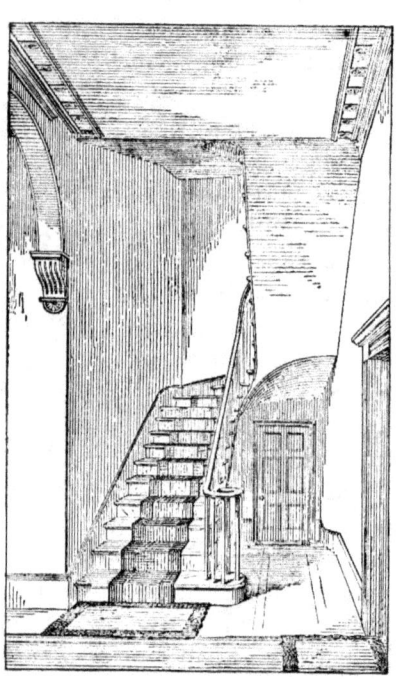

Diagram of a staircase as the builder left it.

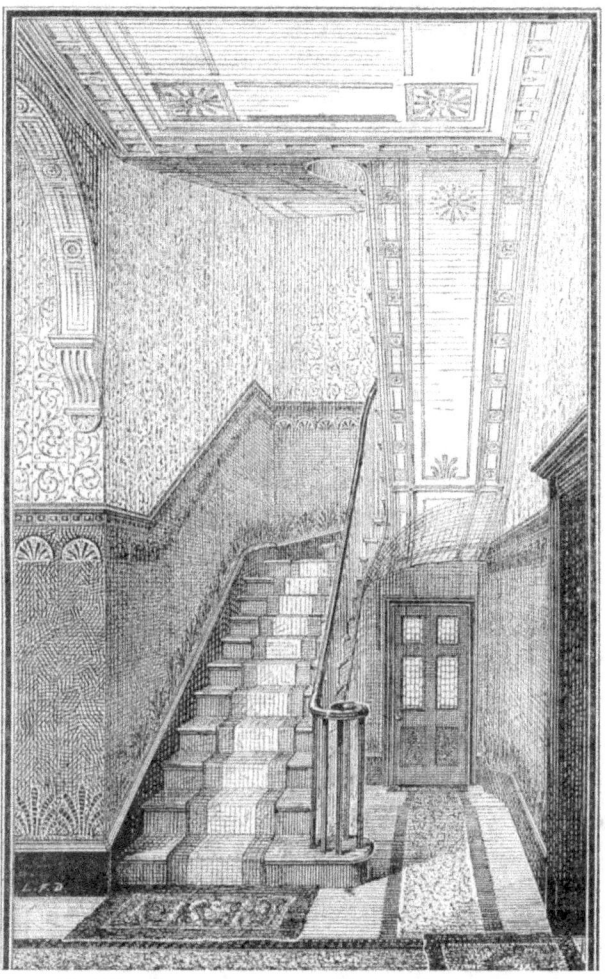

Design showing a simple solution of the difficulty of decorating
a builder's staircase.

the point of view of the diners. In the other case, the dinner-table is, so to speak, only an incident in the furniture, and the decoration must be such as one can live with without weariness or surfeit.

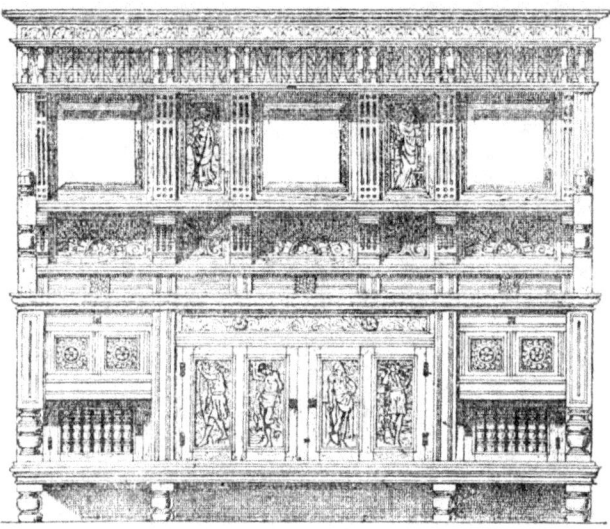

Dining-room sideboard.

About the most uncomfortable of sitting-rooms is that which has been furnished strictly as a dining-room ; and few mistakes are more common than that of adopting the orthodox dining-room " suite " for a room that may be, indeed, a dining-room, in the sense that you dine there, but is more essentially the room in which you live.

One might so decorate a dining-room as to

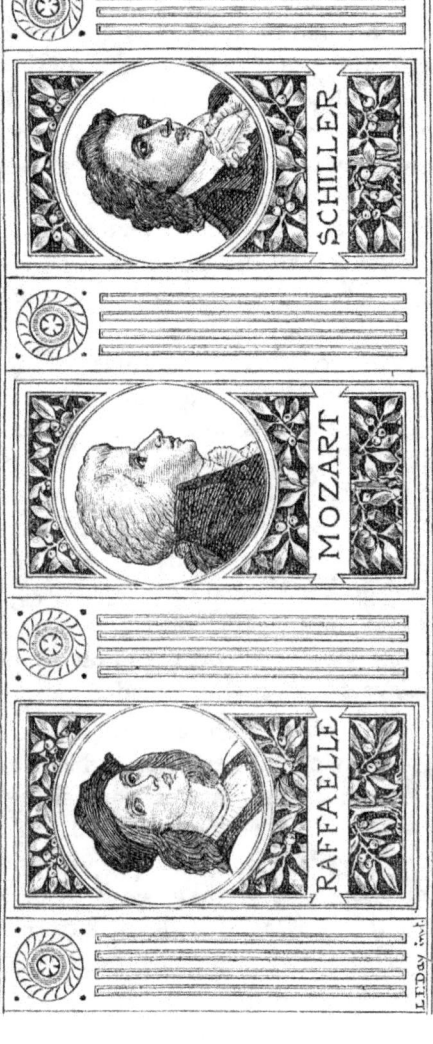

Frieze decoration.

illustrate with some completeness the *menu* of an elaborate dinner, and that without of necessity lapsing into vulgarity ; but such a notion would need to be very judiciously carried out ; and, whatever the delicacy of the artist, the room would be fit only to dine in. Such decoration would be, on the whole, more suitable in a restaurant than in the home of folk who did not devote a great part of their lives to the consideration of what they should eat and drink.

The drawing-room, if it be indeed a drawing-room, should be light and easily illuminated, delicate, and not too serious in its general tone. In the selection of the furniture, the convenience of a number of guests, the facilities for conversation, and so on, have to be consulted. What would make it admirable for its purpose as a drawing-room, would go far to make it unendurable as a dwelling-room ; just as the sparkle that is pleasant in society-talk would be unreal and out of place in intimate conversation by the fireside.

In the living-room let everything radiate from your way of living. There would be little propriety in adorning the walls of your sitting-room with the busts of men who were only names to you, or in writing inscriptions on the walls that had no more meaning to you than the " Mene, Mene " of Scripture to the King of Babylon. Accompanying are illustrations of two schemes of decoration, showing how a man might surround himself in his

Processional frieze of great painters.

home with the effigies of those who were really companions and masters to him. But since it is his home, and not a public building, he should have the courage to admit such as appeal most directly to his sympathies, no matter whether the world allow their supremacy or not; to admit a favourite to the exclusion of a great name; and, if he care more for the lesser poet, to place a Schiller before a Dante—Dante's fame and profile notwithstanding.

> " No profit goes where is no pleasure ta'en ;
> In brief, sir, study what you most affect."

So also in decoration, it is what you most affect that should find a place.

Bed-rooms deserve more thought than is usually bestowed upon them. The "spare-room" excepted, they are not for show, and men grudge expense there accordingly. Yet for the sake of our own self-respect we ought to be as careful concerning our sleeping-rooms as we are about the linen we wear. A fine house with mean bed-rooms is no better than a smart dress and shabby underclothes. The slight esteem in which the sleeping-room is held is illustrated by the common expression that anything better than ordinary is " too good for the bed-room."

Cleanliness is of course a paramount consideration in the arrangement of this room ; and, for the sake of association, there should be more than that;

everything about a bed-room should not only be but look clean. Here, too, the probability of illness has to be thought of. Who has not at some time in his life been confined to a room in which the wall-paper oppressed him like a nightmare? The rosebuds *would* resolve themselves into grotesque faces, peeping out at him from wherever he turned his eyes. Or the pattern became an arithmetical puzzle, never to be solved: when darkness came it brought no relief, and he found himself lying awake half through the night, mechanically counting phantom figures. One such experience as this will go far to convince a man that, in the decoration of many a room, the negative quality of harmlessness is a positive merit.

The richness or poorness of decoration and fur-niture must be proportionate to the means of its possessor. Not that all persons of equal means

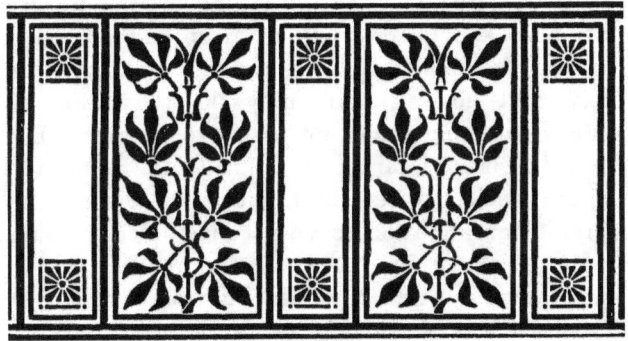

Simple stencilled dado decoration.

need spend equally on their rooms. It must be very much a question with all but the over-rich what interest they take in such things, and what value they attach to them. One man may do wisely in spending a third of his income on objects of art, whilst it would be folly in another to spend a tithe of his. No man is justified in his own eyes in giving more for a thing than it is worth to him. A thing of beauty is not a joy if you are for ever afraid that harm shall happen to it. "There are a hundred ways," wrote Sir Henry Taylor some thirty years ago, "in which luxury overreaches itself—a hundred in which penance enters into the worship of Mammon." In proportion as things become a source of care to us they cease to be a source of pleasure. We smile superior to the bumpkin who walks uneasily in his Sunday suit of black, forgetting that we are equally bumpkins when we array ourselves in garments that we are afraid of soiling, or when we surround ourselves with useful objects that are too fine for use. One may well possess, and enjoy the possession of, things that one could not afford to replace. But if the ordinary wear and tear incidental to the use of an article of dress or furniture be a source of serious consideration to you, it may safely be said to be beyond your means, fit for another and a richer man, but not for you. The folk who fidget about the scratches on the furniture, and the fading of carpets and curtains, would be happier if they had no polished mahogany to be scratched, no rich upholstery to fade. If the occasional breakage of an oriental porcelain cup would be more than a passing annoyance to you, you had better not take your old china into use, but shut it up carefully in a cabinet. Whether the sum of enjoyment to be derived from it would be greater by daily use and occasional loss, or by the consciousness of possession without much risk and loss, is for you to determine.

The superiority of example to precept being proverbial, a practical way of inculcating the principles on which a house should be decorated, will be to take some one room as an instance, and proceed to work out a scheme for its decoration from the very beginning.

In the first place the question is, Who is to inhabit it? What manner of man is he? What are his tastes and habits? For what purpose does he intend the room? We will imagine him a man under middle age, married some years since, his income sufficient for modest comfort, but not adequate to anything like display or luxury. His days are spent away from home. The room to be made pleasant is that in which he mostly spends the evening with his wife. It is a room for rest and quiet. A number of guests is such an unusual event with them that it need not be taken into consideration. The atmosphere of a large party is no more congenial to them intellectually than it is physically, although once or twice in the

year they do their best to be gracious to a number
of worthy people with whom circumstances compel
them to be on friendly terms, but with whom they
have not sufficient sympathy to ask them to spend
an evening at their house alone. The few who
often do pass the evening with them are friends,
familiar because of mutual sympathies. In arranging
the room after their own fashion, therefore, they
will probably be consulting others' comfort as well
as their own; and if not, they will surely make their
friends more comfortable by fulfilling their own
idea than by aiming vainly to carry out theirs.

The room is to be adapted to the habits of its
inmates, and in particular to their evening occupa-
tions. These are various. Sometimes the man
returns from business fagged, and wants rest; or
worried, and wants soothing; or depressed, and
wants rousing. Sometimes the day's work has
scarcely taxed his energies, and he wants to be
doing something. His tastes are perhaps not very
pronounced. He is fond of reading, but not such
an eager reader as to pursue that pleasure under
difficulties. He is no musician, but he has great
pleasure in music, and delights, especially when
he is in the passive mood, to sit and listen to his
wife at the piano. Neither art nor science has
strong attraction for him, but he does like photographs, and has acquired a considerable collection
of them. It is assumed, of course, that the wife is
in sympathy with the husband, or if there be little

differences of idea between them, this is the room
in which his wants prevail, as hers do elsewhere.
(It is simpler to speak always of one person than
two.) Now that we know something of the man
and his habits, it becomes possible to suggest a
reasonable scheme for the arrangement of his room.

As it is chiefly in the evening that this room will
be inhabited, care must be taken not to make it too
dark. That would involve difficulty in the way of
illumination; which means gas; which means heat,
foul air, heaviness, and general discomfort. If a
moderator or duplex lamp or two do not sufficiently
illuminate it, it will be too dark. On the other
hand, it must not be too light, or we shall lose the
feeling of repose, that we most want. Call to mind
the cosiest rooms you can think of, and you will
find that none of them are in a very light key.
They are not white-and-gold drawing-rooms, but
sober morning-rooms, or dining-rooms (so-called)
that are really living-rooms. The tone of the room
then is determined, not so dark as to necessitate
gas, not so light as to appear cold or naked. The
tint is a matter of choice, to be settled according
to preference, or perhaps with reference to the
other rooms; one does not want to have all the
rooms in the house of a colour. The doctor will
be at one with the artist on that point. Before
the distribution of colour and its general arrangement can be determined, we must have some notion
of the general character of the room itself, and

of the more important articles of furniture. It is
of no use, for example, to lavish work on that part
of the wall which will be hidden by furniture or
covered with pictures. Very frequently there will
be some marked feature in the room, an arched
recess perhaps, a moulded ceiling, or a prominent
chimney-piece, that of itself suggests a scheme of
decoration ; or the furniture may do the same.

Since this one room, at least, is to be homely,
let us boldly accept the photographs as worth a
prominent place, if only on account of the owner's
liking for them ; just as we would accept his coins,
his minerals, his butterflies, or any other collection
in which he was deeply interested ; and let these
be the starting-point of the decoration. In selecting enough of these for our purpose we shall choose
the best of course, but not only the best; considerations of proportion, scale, and general effect, will
almost certainly make compromise in the less important pictures desirable. The photographs should
all be framed alike or nearly alike, the difference
in proportion being rectified as much as possible
by more or less of mount ; for it is impossible to
arrange pictures of all shapes and sizes on a wall
with complete satisfaction. The mounts may be
of wainscot, or tinted cardboard, or common brown
paper, or whatever else may harmonise in tone with
the colour of the photographs. The thing to be
most certainly avoided is a white mount. Unless
the walls themselves be uncomfortably light, the

white mounts of pictures catch your eye directly you enter a room, and there is an end to all repose.

As these pictures are to be hung because the owner has pleasure in them, let them be hung where they can be seen, on the eye-line. They may, if there be enough of them worthy of such a position, form a compact band all round the room, interrupted only by the doors, windows, and taller furniture. A further precaution against monotony may be taken by allowing here and there one of the most important frames to rise above the upper line of the picture-band. The lower line will be horizontal, and will correspond with the rail of the dado, which, for reasons partly of use and partly of effect, it will be well to keep considerably darker than the walls above. The darker colour will wear better (and this is the portion of the walls that suffers most from wear), and it will help to connect the furniture and make the place compact and snug. Economy being an object, let us use paper for this dado, choosing a pattern somewhat severe or stiff in style, partly because it seems fit that the base of a wall should be rigid, and partly in order that we may with propriety break out into freer design in the wall above. If we began at the bottom with flowers and scrolls, what should we arrive at by the time we reached the ceiling ? The wall above the pictures is the place for more flowing forms of ornament ; and here again we may as well adopt paper as the simplest, cheapest, and most effective means of giving interest to an expanse of wall. This may be finished off immediately below the cornice by a frieze, deeper or shallower according to the height of the room, very similar in tone, and in character, to the wall-paper. It is commonly believed that such a frieze lowers the room in appearance. If it do so, it is the fault of the contrast in colour, or of the strength of the pattern. A frieze, fitly chosen, serves only to prevent the lines of the wall-paper from seeming to run behind the cornice. There is no reason whatever why it should draw attention to itself. It may even, by connecting the wall surface with the cornice, draw the eye up to the ceiling, and so give the appearance of greater height to a room. On the cornice no labour need be lost in " picking-out " ; all that is wanted is a few shades of intermediate colour, to connect the wall with the ceiling. Should the mouldings be in themselves bald and uninteresting, some stencilled enrichment may be necessary, in order to make up for the shortcomings of the plaster-work. The ceiling is most easily distempered or papered, the colour in either case being a much paler echo of one or two of the colours prevailing on the walls. Crude white is in favour with housewives—"It looks so clean." That is just its fault. It looks so clean, even when it is not, that it makes all else look dirty, even though it may be clean. To paint the flat ceiling of a moderate-sized room by hand is seldom worth while. It is only at great personal inconvenience that one can look long at it, whilst as a matter of fact no one cares to do so. You see it occasionally by accident, and for a moment; and, that that casual glimpse may not be a shock to the eye, it is as well to tint it in accordance with the room, or even cover it with a simple diaper, which will to some extent withdraw the attention from the cracks that frequently disfigure the ceilings of modern houses. What little hand-painting we can afford may best be reserved for the

Painted door-panel.

panels of the doors, window-shutters, and the like, where it can be seen; these doors and the rest of the wood-work being painted in two or three shades of colour, flat or varnished, according as we prefer softness of tone or durability of surface. In this instance the wood-work may as well fall in with the tone of the dado; but this is not a point on which any rule can be laid down. The decoration of the panels should be in keeping with the wall-paper patterns. It may be much more pronounced than they, but still it must not assert itself. A great point of consideration in the decoration of a room is the relation of the various patterns one to another. One has sometimes to sacrifice an otherwise admirable design, simply because nothing else is to be found to go with it. A single pattern, once chosen, will often control the whole scheme of decoration.

Our carpet shall be Persian. Or, better still, there shall be no carpet, but a sufficiency of Persian rugs, distributed as comfort may suggest, the floor of the room being polished, stained and varnished, or even painted, if it be in very bad condition. It is advisable always to have as little carpet about a room as is consistent with warmth. If the table be at all a fixture there is no occasion for a carpet under it. The worst thing one can do is to nail a carpet down over the whole area of the room. There is nothing like a carpet to hold dust. But the rugs can be taken up daily and shaken; and thus, moreover, the wear of brushing is saved. In the pattern of a carpet the chief thing to be sought is unobtrusiveness; colour, too, if it is to be had, but the more blurred and broken the better; anything like definite form is more than dangerous. In many instances a plain colour would answer every decorative purpose, but plain surfaces tell too many tales.

It is time now to think of the furniture; and in choosing it we will consult the actual wants of the persons concerned, and not the prejudices of people in general. Let us have a table large enough for use, and firm enough on its legs to work at, and not a " shaped " table, nor a round one; the former is made to be looked at rather than used, and the latter is fit only for meals or a round game. We must resist the snare of furniture made only for the show-room. On each side of the fireplace may be a low book-shelf, so arranged that, as one sits by the fire, one can always reach a book without effort—a perpetual temptation to reading. Arrangements must be made for books of all kinds, for all moods, some books of reference in particular, and these especially close at hand; on the top of the book-cases let there be candles or a reading-lamp ready; so that there is no excuse for indolence. On the further side of the room will stand a cottage piano, music in this case not being of sufficient importance to warrant the sacrifice of space as well as beauty involved in the admission of a "grand." It appears to be an accepted fact (is it really a fact?) that the fittest shape for a piano is the most hideous. For other furniture, we have a small cabinet for music, and another for photographs; a small movable table that will serve either as work or card table; at least four substantial chairs of the "dining-room" type, in case of a rubber, or if one would do any work at the table; a music chair, a sofa, and half-a-dozen easy-chairs of half-a-dozen different shapes. These last are for passive enjoyment. If you are really in a lazy mood, no one chair is comfortable for long, and your best chance of rest is to change the chair you sit in. The seats may be covered with stuffs of rich and warm effect, all different, but all in harmony; none of them, however, of velvet, like the curtains. The effect of velvet is perfect, and it wears well enough, but it clings too much to answer the purpose of a comfortable seat. Another provision is that none of the material used shall be so costly as to need covering up. The curtains hang from a very simple cornice, or from a brass pole just stout enough to bear them, and fall in straight folds nearly to the ground. They are not looped up; there are no superfluous cords, tassels, or fringes anywhere; there is no millinery about the window. In this room there is no occasion for a looking-glass. The perpetual nuisance of seeing oneself reflected at every turn

in a mirror, more than outweighs any convenience
there might be in it. If such an article had been
necessary, the best thing would have been to frame
it after the manner of the photographs, and hang
it like a picture ; only out of the way, so that
one could not see oneself in it without deliberate
intention.

The clock, which hangs in the corner, is of
brass, and so are the door-handles and other little
fittings, the fender, fire-irons, and coal-scuttle.   It
so happens that the candlesticks and other objects
on the mantelshelf are also of brass.   Not that
it follows because one thing is brass that all the
other things should be of the same ; but even the
little knick-knacks in a room should go together ;
they should not look as though they had met by
accident.   So with the style of the furniture in
our typical apartment.   It does not all come from
one workshop, and certainly it is not what is commercially called "a set," or more grandiloquently,
"*en suite*" ; but whether it be light or heavy, florid
or severe, it has some character, and that character
pervades everything.   All is substantial, too, and
well made, the first expense of good workmanship
being counterbalanced by the saving effected in
doing without all that was not really wanted.
Even the most economically disposed of "those
about to furnish" start with a preconceived idea
that they must have many things for which they
have no use, and no excuse but custom.   Nowhere

is there in our apartment any sham construction
or excrescent ornament. The chairs and sofa show
their framing, and are comfortably padded; they
are not overgrown bolsters with iron entrails. It
is a popular superstition to suppose that the most
apoplectic-looking chairs are the easiest; but, in
truth, it is the *form* of a chair, and not its padding, that has most to do with ease. The maker's
preference for formlessness is easily explained; it
hides all sins of construction, and good joinery is
costly. No one who knows what a well-cut garment is, will put much faith in the tailor or dressmaker who insists upon the supreme efficacy of
padding. That is the panacea of the incompetent.

Imagine now our interior furnished and finished;
not completely, for under no circumstances will a
room, fresh from the hands of the decorator, be
quite free from the suggestion of paint and polish;
only after a few weeks' wear will it begin to look
homely. The occupants, too, will be sure to find
that sundry contrivances for comfort and convenience have been overlooked. If, when these
have been supplied, and the different members of
the scheme have had time to mingle together and
be on friendly terms all round, the effect should
be still unsatisfactory, it can only be through
an entire misapprehension of the wants of the
imaginary indweller. But this is certain; if he
is once satisfied with a room furnished on the
principles here advocated, it will continue to grow

in his affections, and he will become more and
more loth to make any serious alteration in it as
the years go on.

These principles are capable of the widest possible application. Suppose the owner of the room
had been of a more bookish turn of mind. It
would have been easy to modify the same scheme
to suit his tastes. On the following page is shown
something of the sort. In place of photographs,
books occupy the most important place in the
room. The shelves form a decorative feature
round the room, fixed at a level most convenient
for use, high enough to allow chairs to be set
back against the wall under them (in that way
economising space), and low enough to form a broad
shelf, available for purposes either of use or ornament. The wall-space above still affords room for
a few pictures, more particularly such as are bold
enough in style to look well at a certain distance
from the eye; and over the mantel-piece, where
the book-shelves could not conveniently be carried,
would be a place of honour more worthily filled by
a work of art than by a sheet of looking-glass. In
the framing of this central painting in the illustration, the simple plan has been adopted (for the sake
of economy) of carrying on the lines of the somewhat common-place mantel-piece that one finds in
ordinary houses; but with greater outlay a much
more important feature might have been made of
this "over-mantel." The corner of the room, where

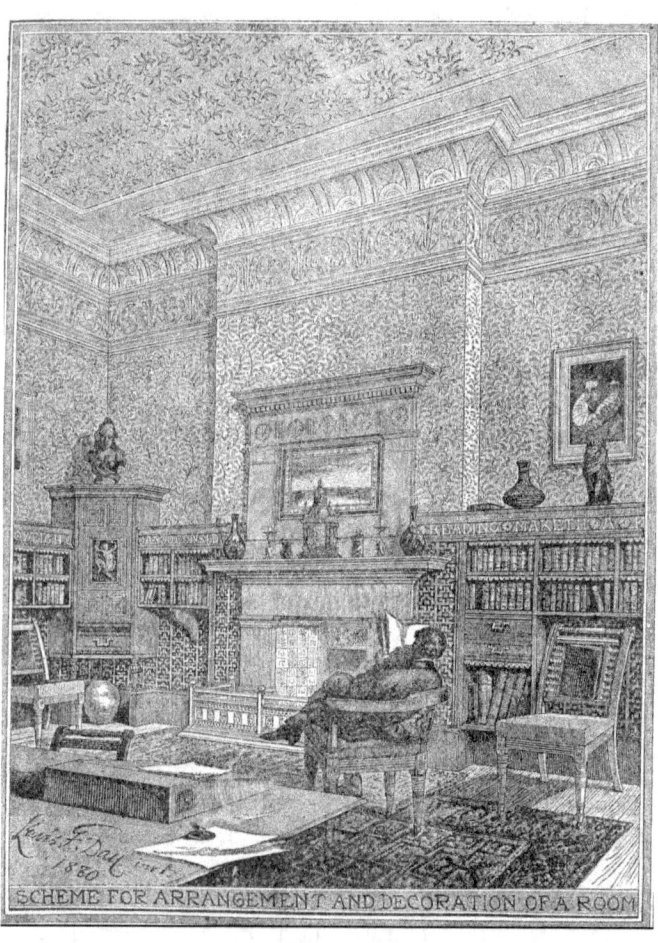

SCHEME FOR ARRANGEMENT AND DECORATION OF A ROOM

some space would be wasted if the shelves were allowed to meet at right angles, is just the place for a useful cupboard, and the door-panel of such a prominent piece of furniture is well adapted for a decorative figure, inlaid or painted, as the case may be ; for it faces the owner as he sits in his easy-chair by the fire, his feet on the fender, which, by the way, has a bar arranged at a convenient height, so that he can toast his toes in comfort, instead of scorching his instep, as he would if the fender were too low. His back is to the light, and he can read with case. On the table at his left is a movable desk, in case he should want to write, and at his right hand the book-case is carried, for once, nearly down to the ground, so as to accommodate the larger books of reference which it is convenient to have near at hand. The inscription on the frieze of the book-case is introduced to show that there is always an opportunity somewhere in a room for the whim or fancy of its inmate.

There is no limit to the schemes of decoration that might be built upon a man's personal ideal. The whole argument is that his ideal should be the basis of the art about him, whatever that ideal may be.

PICTURES IN THE HOUSE.

" How many things by season season'd are
To their right use and true perfection ! "

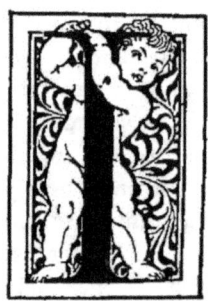

IT is not easy to determine definitely the value of pictures as decoration. The great paintings of the great masters were for the most part painted with a view to decorative effect, and we can scarcely conceive decoration of a higher kind than was executed by Michael Angelo and Paul Veronese. A painting is best seen in its place; and it is art in its place that is best worth seeing. But with the modern practice of easel-painting the probability of pictures being painted for their places is of the slightest ; and as a fact, a large proportion of the pictures that hang on our walls are out of place, and in no sense whatever decorative. And yet it is not too much to say that the prevalent idea of decoration is to hang pictures on the walls—if good, so much the better—but to hang pictures of some sort.

It may be at once conceded that to place good

pictures in good positions, and subordinate the colour of the walls to them, is about as perfect a method of decoration as could be. Good works, however, are scarce, and good places for pictures none too frequent ; although the common practice is, not only to depend upon paintings for furnishing our walls, but to sacrifice everything to them, no matter what their worth or worthlessness.

It is beside the question to draw comparison between pictures and wall-papers. No fanatic will deny that a fine picture is worthy of the front place in decoration, and that all other art should be subsidiary to it. The only question is whether a picture, or a number of pictures collectively, are worth anything at all, and, if worth hanging, whether they are worth the sacrifice of a room to them. A dwelling-room is, after all, a dwelling-room, and not a picture gallery ; and common-sense would dictate that paintings should take their place in the decorative scheme according to the interest and enjoyment the owner has in them. All that is here combatted is the popular prejudice that pictures, as pictures, and without regard to their individual beauty, are essential to, or even preeminent in, a decorative scheme.

The first and most important question to be asked with regard to the introduction of pictures into a room is whether they are worth the sacrifice of the walls to them ; and that is just the question that is almost invariably not asked. It is taken for granted that pictures there shall be. If already acquired, the possession of them is supposed to be reason enough for their display ; and when there are none, the thoughtless assumption that pictures are a matter of course, suffices to insure their early purchase.

The worth of a picture is not to be estimated by its money value, nor even, from the purchaser's point of view, altogether by its intrinsic value as art. If a painting afford genuine pleasure to a man, that is his sufficient reason for the purchase of it, and if he be really a lover of art he will not inquire too closely into its safety as an investment. If pictures on the walls delight a man more than any other kind of art, it would be foolish in him to sacrifice his own satisfaction for the sake of an effect which he does not appreciate. If he really enjoys his pictures, though they be bad, likes to look at them, and does look at them in preference to everything else around him, he is right, from his point of view, to hang them where he can see them, right even to spoil the effect of his room. What needs to be pointed out is that the effect of the room is very likely to be spoiled by them ; and that a vast number of people encumber their walls with pictures, which are not only of no merit whatever, but for which they personally do not really care in the least, and at which they never look. Unconsciously they sacrifice decorative effect to what is neither preference nor conviction, but simply habit.

They are accustomed to pictures, and a room without them appears to be bare. Naturally, if you take down so much as a single frame from its accustomed place, the space will assert its emptiness. If you all at once leave off wearing a favourite ring, the finger for a while feels naked. It does not follow from the fact of the eye, accustomed to look on walls well furnished with frames, missing them if they are not there, that therefore there is nothing so satisfactory and restful to the eye as pictures.

Good paintings are priceless; and the enjoyment of mediocre ones may be worth more than good decoration which one is not fitted by temperament or education to enjoy. But pictures are not indispensable to the furnishing of a room. Even the best present difficulties in the way of fitting them into the general scheme of the room, or of inventing a scheme to fit them; often the pictures themselves are not in tune together; and very frequently all choice lies between pictures and decorative oneness, the two being incompatible.

Let no one take it for granted that he must purchase pictures, nor yet that, having them, he is bound to display them. The safer rule would be to hang no picture but what is really cared for. And from what a world of trash that would relieve us !

It is not here the question of a picture gallery, but of the enlivening and enrichment of a living-

room with pictures. To introduce a great number
of pictures into an ordinary room, without detri-
ment either to their effect or that of the room, is impossible. To dot the walls all over, from skirting to
cornice, with canvases of all shapes and sizes, in all
sorts of frames, is excusable only in a public exhibition, and is there only a qualified evil. If the pictures be worth hanging, hang them in a good light
and where they can be appreciated. Few of us are
so fortunate as to be embarrassed by the possession
of more fine works of art than we can conveniently
hang "on the line" in our rooms; and those few
may be presumed to be in a position to build themselves a gallery. If we bear in mind the arbitrary
and various shapes and sizes of pictures, and the
equally arbitrary proportions of the walls, as well
as the all-important but inevitable positions of the
windows, the difficulties in the way of introducing
many pictures into a decorative scheme with happy
effect will be obvious.

The most favourable conditions under which
pictures may with advantage be introduced into
decoration are, where a few good pictures already
exist (not more than can be exhibited in a fair
light), and the decorator has only to work up to
them—throwing them individually into sufficient,
but not too great, prominence, whilst connecting
them into one complete and unpretentious whole.

Where there are no pictures, it is not a bad plan
so to arrange the lines of decoration that certain

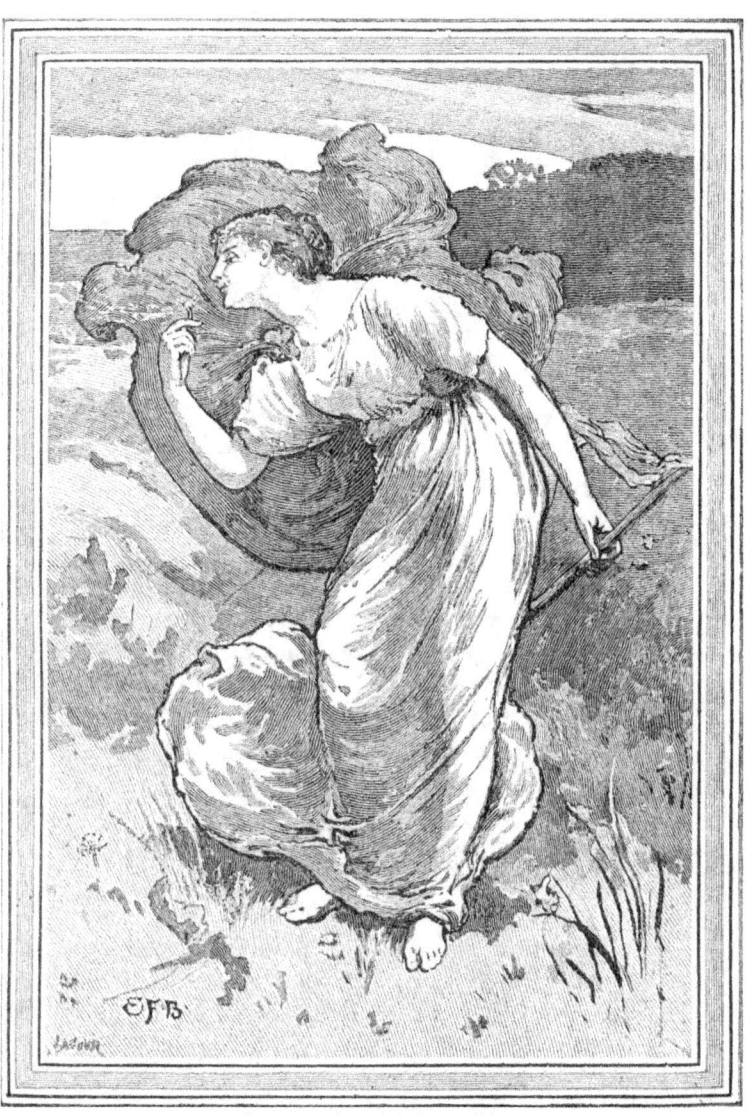

Decorative picture-panel.

prominent panels, or other spaces, are left for pictures of a more or less decorative character. But this implies two things ; first, that the painter is prepared to submit to the slight limitations imposed on him by the decorative intention in the room, and to paint in sympathy with it ; second, that the patron is prepared to give the painter a commission. Most men prefer to see a picture before they buy it.

Instead of pictures being, as is supposed, the simplest solution of the decorative problem, the difficulty of assimilating them is such that, on the whole, the best plan is to content oneself with very few indeed, and those only of the best, substituting for the rest more careful and thoughtful decoration. Where good pictures are, on account of their costliness, out of the question, good decoration is usually within reach—so near, in fact, that it is apt to be overlooked. But it offers no security, real or imagined, of investment; and many a man hesitates, therefore, to spend the odd shillings in decoration where he lavishes guineas upon paintings.

It is not often that pictorial art, and that the best of its kind, is altogether unattainable. Photographs have the unpardonable fault that they fade before our eyes, grow paler, and dimmer, and yellower, and ghastlier, as the days go on, until only the horrid ghost of the picture that pleased us confronts us in its place. Still, there are photographic processes that claim to be permanent ; there is etching,

which gives the work of the artist at first-hand ;
there are mezzotints ; and, lastly, there are wood-
engravings, almost perfect in their way, and only
so cheap that they are not thought to be worth
framing.

Our reverence for a painting in oil has in it something approaching to superstition. How few persons
think of adorning their walls with anything else !
Our hearts are set on cabinet pictures, and we
spend more on a single second-rate, if not worthless, painting, than would suffice to line our walls
with works of real though less pretentious art.
Why is this so ? Is it the colour that attracts ?
Not altogether that. If colour were the charm,
we should find enamels and embroideries, at once
more gorgeous and less costly than paintings, exhibited in honourable positions on the walls, where
they could be seen. It cannot be the subject
that is esteemed, for that is common also to every
form of engraving. The pride of possession may
account for it in some degree. There is a pleasure
in possessing what is unique ; and the perpetual
repetition of a beautiful thing does deprive it, if
not of its beauty, of some of its charm. Probably
the chief attraction lies in the prestige attached
to picture painting, a prestige altogether beyond
its deserts. If the value of art is not merely as
decoration, neither does it consist in immortalising
dead herrings or living nobodies. Rich hangings
and fine furniture are perhaps as well worth having

as the painted "texture" of silk and satin, and the costume, that go to make many a picture. A picture is only worthy of the first place in proportion to its worthiness among pictures ; a painting as such is not necessarily above ornament, nor available as ornament ; and a whole collection of inferior paintings has nothing like the charm of a simple room that has been decorated with adequate art.

There was a time when all painting was more or less decorative ; now it is for the most part very far removed from anything of the kind. Not only painting and sculpture (which we are accustomed to dignify by the title of "fine" art) but also decorative art, appeal in the first instance to the eye ; and their first, if not their highest, duty is to satisfy the eye. So far their ambition is the same. But neither of them stops there. Each attempts something more than that, and it is in this ulterior effort that their paths diverge. The further they go, the wider they wander apart. Fine art seeks, beyond the satisfaction of the eye, to express some thought or sentiment, some feeling or impression, perhaps some dream or aspiration of the artist. Decorative art has, over and above beauty, and even before beauty, to fulfil some useful purpose. Sometimes, indeed, to beauty and the expression of himself the painter adds a decorative element, by adapting his design to some special purpose, as when he paints a picture with a view to the particular position it is to occupy; and sometimes the decorator puts into his work such meaning or such feeling as to raise it to a level with fine art, be it ever so fine ; but the distinction is for the most part only too broadly defined, and it is seldom that one need hesitate whether to describe a work as a painting treated decoratively or as a decorative panel.

Some painters there are whose bias is in the direction of decoration, who would have been decorators, but for the accident of their education, or the low esteem in which decorative art was held in the days of their pupilage. The work of such men is, whether they will it or not, decorative, and falls into its place in decoration quite easily and naturally ; whereas the art of the born *painter* is not content with any place, even the highest, is not content to be first, but will be all and everything. Art is decorative in proportion as it can be reconciled with its surroundings.

It is scarcely necessary to say that if the various paintings on the walls of a room are to contribute to its decorative effect, there should be some sort of accord between them, both in colour and proportion ; but it is worth while to remark that their effect from any and every probable point of view should be taken into account. Do they form patches of pleasant colour or of interesting black-and-white as you sit in your arm-chair and look at the wall before you, without being quite aware that you are looking at it ? Very possibly you see more of them from that point of view than from the nearer standpoint from which they deserve attention. If it is only from that nearer point that they please, they can hardly be said to contribute to the decoration of the walls they occupy.

About the most difficult of paintings to be brought into decoration are family portraits ; and yet it would not only be a waste of words, but would betray some want of feeling, to suggest their summary exclusion from the family circle to which they belong by right of affection or sentiment. As a matter of practice we find that family feeling proves strong enough to counteract the weakness of even the weakest art of the portrait painter. Nor is this to be regretted. But it is a pity that where no excuse of feeling exists, and it is merely a question between art and custom, art should so inevitably have the worst of it.

If what has been said above concerning the unfitness of so many pictures for any decorative purpose is true, still more certain is it that modern sculpture contributes scarcely at all to decorative art. Spectral busts and ghosts of classic gods may haunt, with some propriety, the galleries in mansions of a day gone by ; but there is no place in the house of an Englishman of modest means and unpretending establishment for sculpture, as it appears to be understood by the sculptors of this generation. They are accustomed to complain of the scant patronage of their art. If they were but content to call themselves carvers, a title of which no man was ashamed in the days when the art was alive and flourishing, they might add their share to the sum of every-day art. They would find it, moreover, not only immediately profitable, but the surest training for work worthy of the name of sculpture—if indeed the Latinised term be in any sort the more dignified.

The ideal way of introducing pictures into the decoration of a room is to have them painted for the prominent places they are to occupy. The actual practice of to-day is quite contrary to this. Permanent decoration is rather shunned than sought. We seem to be reverting to the original type, and becoming more and more nomadic in our mode of life. The modern notion of a dwelling-house is something very far removed from an epic in stone or an idyll in brick; rather it takes the shape of a roof over one's head and a momentary resting-place. We may not be altogether satisfied with this as a solution of the building question, but neither can we ignore the fact that we live in an age when things appear to be in that state of transition which does not encourage art of anything like a monumental character. If the house of the future is to be only a kind of more substantial tent, cabinet pictures will form the most portable, and therefore the fittest, decoration for it.

In hanging pictures in a room we have to consider

two things—the pictures and the room. A painter
might, perhaps, be found rash enough to say that
only the pictures deserve to be taken into consideration ; but no artist would say so. That the room
alone should be thought of, is an absurdity beyond
the conception even of a nineteenth-century æsthete.
Whether the effect of the pictures or of the room is
of more importance, will depend upon the quality of
the pictures and the value attached to them by the
owner. But the very fact that pictures are to be
hung pre-supposes that they are, in the owner's eyes
at least, worth hanging ; and, that being so, they
ought by no means to be sacrificed to the general
decorative effect. If they were of no more importance than that, the whole advice to those who con-
templated hanging them would best be summed up
in the recommendation, not to do anything of the
kind.

Assuming that pictures are to be hung, we must
assume also, for argument's sake, however little
the assumption may be justified by the facts, that
the owner is interested in them and would like to
see them to advantage. The question is, how can
he best manage this without sacrificing the room to
them altogether ? He may well want to have pictures about him without being prepared to make
them his only care, however good they may be. It
resolves itself into this :—How, in a moderate-sized
room, lighted probably from one side by one or
more windows, which do not extend quite up to the

cornice, the walls pierced by one or more doors, and in places occupied by necessary furniture, *so* to arrange a certain number of pictures that individually each is placed in a good light, and collectively they contribute to the decorative effect of the room ?

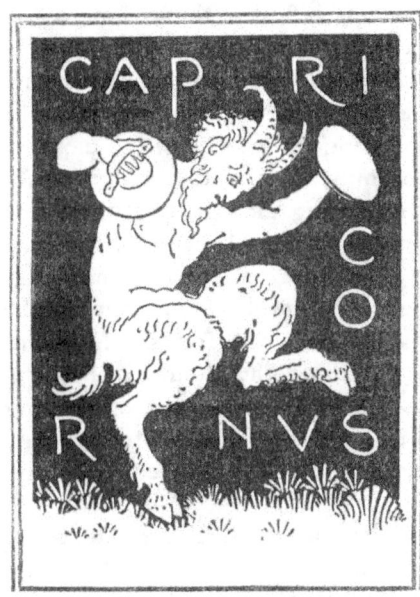

Strongly defined decorative panel.

The first step towards a solution of the difficulty will be, to inquire as to how much of the wall-space is sufficiently lighted : that alone is available for pictures. Decoration may be painted in any key, subdued in the light to utmost tenderness, or forced up, in dark corners, to a pitch of brightness that would be unendurable in ordinary daylight ; the dancing Capricornus above is so strongly defined that his form will not be lost in the darkest shadow ; but a picture, in order to be seen, must be in a good light, and it is a cruel injustice to the artist to hang it in any other.

A room may be so situated that light is reflected into it in the most unexpected manner. It may, for example, face a white wall on which the sun shines brightly, and is reflected thence on to the ceiling in such a way that it is the lightest part of the room ; but as a rule it is the darkest, and, equally as a rule, when we take into account the lighting of the walls and the security of the pictures, there is in a room only a horizontal band of wall-space between the ceiling and the floor fit for the hanging of pictures. This band is further removed from the ceiling than from the floor. The centre of it is just above the level of the eye of the spectator as he stands, say five feet six inches or six feet from the ground. The blunder of hanging pictures too high is as common as that of hanging them too low is rare. Whoever hesitates between two levels will be tolerably safe in deciding upon the lower.

It will be all the better both for the room and the paintings, if they can be confined to a single row. They will then, of course, be fixed on the exact level that suits them, and the eye will not be diverted to other works above or below them. Whether there be room, however, for two or three tiers of frames, will depend upon the height of the room, the light, and the size of the works themselves. It is not often that there is

space for a triple band, even where the works are
small. The smaller they are the less will they
bear to be removed very far from the eye. Now
and then a bolder painting than the rest will hold
its own, even when placed above the line that suits
them ; and such a deviation from the formal
arrangement prescribed by practical considerations,
forms a welcome break in the monotony of the wall
surface ; but for the most part, if pictures are to be
seen, and well seen, they must be on the line of
sight. The danger of sameness in this arrangement is not so great as might be feared. The
picture band cannot under any circumstances run
right round the room. Not only do windows,
doors, and furniture intervene, but there are spaces
between the windows, and at their sides, as well as
in the angles of the room, into which the light does
not penetrate fully, where it would be sheer waste
to hide pictures. On the wall opposite the light,
also, there is usually a space, more especially if
there be two windows and consequent cross lights,
where a painting is not fairly seen, and where it
would be better to place a mirror, or a cabinet, or
whatever else may be convenient.

There is in most rooms less wall-space fit for oil
paintings than for water-colours. The latter, being
usually brighter and purer in colour, absorb less
light, and are less difficult to place. Water-colours,
moreover, are, by consent of custom, more habitually
placed in the drawing-room, a light room in itself,

where the pictures are chiefly seen by what we still call " candle-light," though it is commonly gas; so that the consideration of daylight effect is of less consequence. If there be injustice to the art of the water-colour painter, in thus assuming that his works may with propriety be placed so as best to be seen by a light for which they were not painted, the injustice is on the part of those who so place them. It is not fair to a fine picture to banish it to a room where you seldom sit by day. But neither is it altogether reasonable, if you do hang paintings in a room that you only inhabit by night, to hang them according to the light under which you never see them. The man who has purchased a picture usually thinks that, when he has paid for it, he owes nothing to the artist, and that he is at liberty to put it to the use that best pleases himself. We cannot expect of all men the sentiment of gratitude to the painter, or of tenderness for his repute. If a busy man has little or no opportunity of enjoying his treasures of art by day, should he therefore be debarred from the pleasure of possessing them ? All things considered there may be just excuse for hanging pictures where they will only be seen by night ; but fuller justice will naturally be done to them, and fuller enjoyment of course afforded by them, when they are so arranged as to be seen under the most favourable conditions of ordinary daylight.

An important consideration is the treatment of the wall-space between the frames. The character

or colour that best suits pictures is not at all as
a matter of course that which is most desirable
for the rest of the wall surface. Almost as a rule
it will be convenient to have a slightly darker
colour below the pictures; indeed the dado may
often be considerably deeper in colour. Where the
tint that forms the background to the pictures is
best carried up to the cornice, the *pattern*, which is
appropriate as a mere filling between the frames,
may be too insignificant and uninteresting for the
breadth of wall above. A very good plan is to
separate the picture belt from the upper and lower
wall spaces by simple mouldings of wood, and the
more deliberately we do this the more safely we
can treat it with reference to the pictures. The
colour that helps them may absorb so much light
that, if it were carried all over the walls, we should
feel the want of the rays that a lighter upper wall
would reflect. On the other hand the light wall
colour, that alone would make white picture mounts
endurable, would in many instances be too cold
and naked-looking as it neared the floor, and
every article of furniture stood out in sharp relief
against it.

Painters differ as to the colour that is safest as a
background for oil paintings. Deep dull red was
for many years the tone most in vogue; of late
there has been a reaction in favour of neutral green.
A yellowish brown, as nearly as possible the equivalent to gold in shadow, serves the purpose admira-

bly ; some shades of the common brown paper used
for parcels, are not far removed from the colour
that is meant, and artists have sometimes dared to
cover the walls on which pictures hang with that very
material. Whatever the colour adopted, it is easier
to arrive at a satisfactory effect by "breaking" it.
This is easily done by the use of a somewhat vague
pattern in a tint only slightly removed from the
ground. What is known as a damask pattern will
suggest the character of design. This may be
either stencilled or printed, according as the wall
is painted or papered. Anything more than stencilling as a background to pictures would be extravagance ; and by stencilling the softest effects
of diapering may be produced. An artist will
sometimes dab down part of the pattern here
and there, leaving it blurred, indistinct, occasionally
almost obliterated, so producing an effect of softly
varied colour that could be produced by no merely
mechanical process. What is known as "painted
flock" serves also admirably as a background. This
has most of the artistic advantages without the
disadvantages which medical science has discovered
in the ordinary flock. It is, in the first instance,
flock-paper, only printed three or four times over,
until the pattern is raised considerably above the
ground. After it is fixed on the walls it is painted.
The flock absorbs several coats of paint, but when
once that is well dry it is as hard as the wall itself,
and may be scrubbed if necessary. It has the

economic advantage that at any time a coat of
paint will bring it back to its original freshness,
and the artistic merit that the inequality of its
surface ensures "broken " colour ; the pattern is
sufficiently shown without asserting itself.

If only the picture band is to be treated, it would
really not be a great extravagance to *gild* the wall
between the pictures. This is at once the most
obvious way of connecting gold frames, the richest
decoration for the walls, and the most sympathetic
setting for pictures. If the surface of the wall were
first sanded, or in any other way roughened, the
effect would not appear too. gorgeous, when the
pictures were tolerably close together. And there
would not be much of it to be done. There would
be no occasion to gild the wall behind the pictures.
As a principle of decoration one would not advo-
cate the leaving undone any small wall-space that
might be hidden ; but the filling up of the interstices
between pictures is not quite the same thing as the
scamping of wall-spaces that may not be seen. It
might be as well to diaper such a gold ground as
has been described ; or the entire wall might be
painted gold-colour, and only the spaces between
the frames diapered with a pattern in gold. In
a drawing-room in which the pictures are set in
gold frames with white mounts, the wall surface
about them might be white, or white and gold, the
space above being still white with ornament in
delicate shades of pure colour. These might be

tolerably bright without much danger of offence, for the shadow in which the cornice and upper walls are thrown would soften them considerably.

One can conceive an effect of decoration where the pictures are so closely put together (exhibition fashion) that they form a kind of Venetian mosaic in which the slabs are not of marble but of canvas.   But it would be a degradation of the art

of the painter to reduce it to the value of a mere patch of colour on the wall, and a needless one when that effect may be produced by such very simple means indeed. The appearance of lavishness may sometimes be gratifying, but the evidence of waste is always offensive.

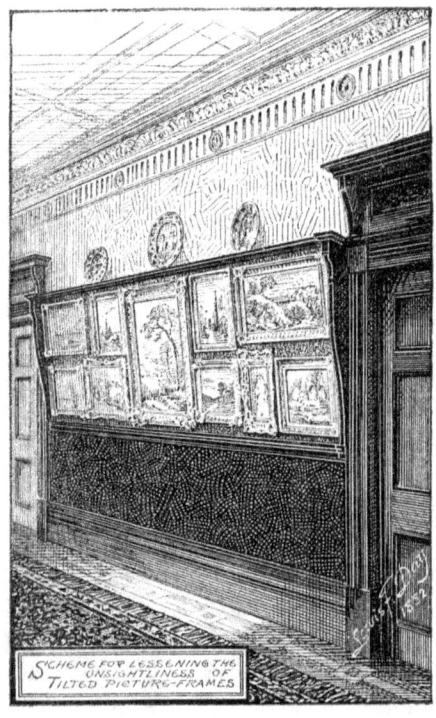

SCHEME FOR LESSENING THE UNSIGHTLINESS OF TILTED PICTURE-FRAMES

The custom still lingers among us of tilting pictures forward. So placed, they get some advantage in the matter of light, but at a cost to the effect of the room that is seldom justified. It must be indeed a fine picture that will excuse the overhanging frame. Where a great number of pictures are concerned, it might be worth while to try the experiment of a sloping wall space between the dado and upper wall. The pictures placed upon this would not individually have the unpleasant effect of falling forward, and the frames would not cast gigantic shadows on the wall. The slight slope of the wall itself would probably be scarcely noticeable. There would, it is true, be a ledge above it, which might be gratefully accepted as an opportune shelf for porcelain, terra-cotta, and the like, or condemned from the beginning as a "dust trap," according as one were bitten with the æsthetic or the sanitary mania. But this last objection might be overcome at the sacrifice of a few inches of the room, by bringing the wall above it forward. This would necessitate a new cornice to the room, the old one being hidden ; but it is not often that a room is crowned with a cornice that we need have any qualms about sacrificing ; and the expense of the whole business would be slight. Of course there would needs be a cornice-like moulding, perhaps gilded, to mark the termination of the picture band, as well as a chair rail below it. If these were skilfully managed the transition from perpendicular to slanting could scarcely offend, and the pictures would certainly benefit by the expedient. The real difficulty would be at the doors and windows. The consideration of expense might stand in the way of the experiment being tried ; but it would not be a very ruinous operation. In comparison with the cost of a single picture, it would be quite inappreciable. One is inclined to marvel how a man who pays princely prices for paintings can be so little princely as to begrudge them a fair setting. But wonder ceases when we reflect how few pictures are bought for the love of them, how few come into the possession of those who appreciate them at their real value, without reference to the name of the painter or the security of the investment.

The framing of pictures is a subject on which most men have their own opinions. Some painters take great pains to get frames that accord with their work, some seem not to trouble themselves about the matter the least in the world. Very few concern themselves about the effect of the frame in the room, their interest being limited to the appearance of their own work. Yet surely the decorative effect of the room is worth a thought. In the case of pictures that have a somewhat decorative character, it is a comparatively simple matter to devise a frame that is in harmony, both with them and the room. The frames, for example, of Sir Frederick Leighton, are all that a decorator could desire ; the difficulty is with regard to the works of the more realistic painters, whose ideal is force, and who think of a frame only as a means of enhancing the effect of atmosphere, perspective, light, life, or whatever may be their aim. This is best done by a boldly projecting frame, the mouldings of which retire by steep degrees from the spectator. There would be no harm in that, but for the fact that, since there must be a limit to the width of the frame, if the greater part of it has been taken up by these retiring members there is no room left for an equally consistent treatment of the frame as it approaches the wall. Sometimes the outer edge of the frame is allowed to project straight out from the wall like a box, without any attempt to mitigate its harshness. Where the pictures are placed so close together that the frames touch one another, this is all very well ; but if a picture is to be hung separately, its frame should seem to belong to the wall and not appear to be stuck on to it. It should by rights look almost as if it grew there. The mouldings, that is to say, should advance by shallow and easy steps from the wall to the most prominent member, and thence, if you will, retire steeply and suddenly to the picture level. This applies, it will be understood, to comparatively heavy frames ; those that consist to a great extent of flat mount offer no difficulty. A round or oval, or other non-rectangular frame, is a sort of bull in a picture gallery, and makes havoc with all the rest.

It is assumed that picture frames will be gilded. Some French painters have made admirable use of black frames, but it takes an artist, and an experienced one, to know just what picture will gain by such framing.

The mouldings of a frame may not inappropriately be interrupted by rosettes or square blocks, which are more particularly valuable when the lines are somewhat too long ; but some little nicety is required in arranging these stops at proper intervals, and accordingly the frame composed of simple mouldings prevails.

The indulgence in fancy frames is dangerous. Sober Englishmen need scarcely be warned against eccentricities such as were exhibited in the Italian gallery at Paris in 1878. Frames, rough as a birds'-nest, with reptiles and other creatures in all the high relief of life, the body of a snake actually projecting in front of the canvas, reach a point beyond our insular idea of realism. Nor is there often to be seen (what was actually exhibited in the same section) an instance of the flat mount, which would naturally form part of the frame, being in reality *painted* on the picture itself, so that the artist could perform the trick of making a goose in the immediate foreground seem absolutely to be stretching its neck out of the picture, and in front of the frame.

Still even in England there is a danger of tasteless extravagance ; witness the frame of a portrait by an eminent and earnest painter, exhibited in

the Grosvenor Gallery not long since, on which
were modelled the branches of an apple tree tinted
in imitation of nature. Not content with fruit and
foliage, the artist represented even the *section* of
an apple, with core and pips complete. It is to
be hoped there was in all this, some symbolic
intention which (to the painter at least) excused
this eccentricity. To the ordinary observer there
was in it nothing but absurdity. The wilfulness
of Mr. Whistler is qualified by a remarkably keen
sense of the values of colour, and most of his
pictures owe something to the fit framing that he
has devised for them. But even he is not always
quite happy in his departure from the safe ground
of common-place; and a word of warning may
perhaps be necessary to some who might aspire to
follow his seductive example without possessing his
faculty. Words of warning are for the most part
only words wasted ; but the fear of being ridiculous
is always a powerful check on us, and it is as well
to hold up that fear before the imagination of those
who contemplate the fantastic framing of pictures.

Much of what has been said about frames applies
to mounts. The choice between white and gold is not
wide, and one may well feel some natural impatience
at such restraints as these limits impose. Many a
picture would be seen to best advantage in a
mount tinted especially to suit it ; but the choice
of a tinted mount is at all times a very delicate
matter, and only actual experiment will determine

what best suits the painting. A tint that will suit all the pictures in a room would be difficult indeed to decide, unless they had been chosen with a view to decorative oneness; and the juxtaposition of a number of variously tinted mounts with reference to the pictures individually, and not to the *ensemble* of the room, could not but produce a patchy and unpleasant appearance.

It might be rash to say that one's choice must, therefore, lie absolutely between white and gold; but it is quite safe to assert that every departure from the accepted alternative is really venturesome. If you are confident of your own judgment in such a matter, and especially of your own patience, dare, by all means, and you may do something decorative. But if you have any doubt of your own nice discrimination, or if you wish to spare yourself vexation and trouble, the wiser course is to submit yourself resignedly to the tyranny of the conventional. It may be consolatory to reflect that there is usually some substantial reason for the common acceptance of a custom, even though it be no higher or worthier than the laziness which tempts us to shirk trouble.

Painters very frequently prefer white mounts for water-colour drawings, and perhaps the white mount is in most cases best for the picture. Certainly the gold mount is best for the effect of the room, or rather it is much more easily brought into a decorative scheme. White mounts, in gold frames, almost compel the adoption of white-and-gold as the key-note of the decoration. Not all the common-place that has been perpetrated in that much abused combination, can alter the fact that there is something refined and delicate in it. Something is yet to be done in white-and-gold, perhaps ; but at its best it is fit only for a drawing-room, fitter for a drawing-room of the period when " evening dress " was not understood to mean, that ladies and gentlemen should array themselves as if to emphasise what contrast there may be between the sexes, but when men and women vied with each other in the brightness of the stuffs they wore, the richness of the lace, the delicacy of the embroidery. We are wiser, perhaps, than the gentlemen of the reign of Queen Anne, but we are less in place in a drawing-room of the style of Louis Quatorze ; and, even were it not so, we have had enough, for a little while to come, of white-and-gold ; nausea has followed on satiety, and the taste of the day revolts against it. With it we must, unless we sacrifice everything to the pictures, give up white mounts. Gold mounts offer a sort of compromise between the claims of the pictures and those of the room. If one simple rule as to the mounting of water-colours could possibly be laid down it would be : " Adopt dull gold mounts "; but at the end of every such dogmatic rule one feels tempted to add :— " *quod est absurdum.*"

For photographs, if they may be included among

"pictures," a mount of unpolished wainscot is as good as anything can be. Prints were mounted in the days of our grandfathers on tinted paper, with parallel lines ruled on the mount as a sort of finish. The modern collector's pride in his proof before letters is, perhaps, responsible for the white mounts that usually stare us in the face when we enter a gentleman's library.

Something remains to be said as to the manner in which pictures should be attached to the walls. There are various kinds of "patent picture line" which answer the purpose well enough, and need no advertisement. But it will be as well to reduce the use of any of them to a minimum. If the wall space be subdivided in the manner already advocated, the pictures may well be hung from the moulding which tops the picture band. It is a simple matter to make this moulding of such a section, that a hook of bent brass wire is all that is necessary to obviate the nuisance of knocking nails into the wall. The upper part of it grips the moulding, whilst to the lower, the cord is attached. The arrangement has this advantage, too, that one can so easily slide the hooks along, and adjust the picture wherever one will—no slight convenience when one is arranging pictures. A frame is best hung by two perpendicular cords, instead of by a single cord which slants to right and left from a nail. That, it may be said, is a matter of taste ; but there is this in favour of the perpendicular lines, that they

are less likely to attract attention ; and that, if they
do catch the eye, they fall in more naturally with
the constructional lines one is accustomed to, and
expects to find there. Where it happens to be
more convenient to fix the pictures to the wall by
means of nails, the painted flock-paper already
mentioned will prevent the plaster from crumbling
away at the first blow of the hammer, and the nail
holes, never very obvious in it, will easily be made
good. But if once you are sure of the place the
picture should occupy, you need not hesitate to
drive in nails pretty recklessly. The wall will be
spoilt by the picture if not by them ; it will be
rubbed where the frame comes in contact with it,
and the space that is not exposed to the light will
not change colour with the rest of the wall ; so that
when the pictures are removed or rearranged the
wall will, in any case, have to be made good.

Pictures might more often than they are be
attached by little metal plates, such as are used to
fix mirrors and wall brackets. The projection of
the frame would hide them, and the necessity of
cords would be done away with altogether. The
difficulty of attaching pictures in their places,
however, is slight compared to the difficulty of
temporarily arranging them, before it is quite
certain whether that situation will suit them. The
hanging of every picture should be a matter of
actual experiment; mere consideration is not enough.
A wise picture lover would seldom purchase a

picture without having a clear notion of where he could hang it, and trying the affect of it in a light similar to that for which he intended it.

It should be reiterated, in conclusion, that to hang pictures fairly we must strictly limit the number of them in our rooms. Does any one really want his walls plastered with them, like a patchwork of big postage stamps ? It is seldom a man finds at a modern exhibition more than a few pictures that he really and lastingly longs to possess. Of these some prove to be already sold, whilst others are, perhaps, beyond his means ; so that the number of works interesting him intensely, which he can possibly acquire, is reduced to a minimum. It may be some consolation to think that this minimum of pictures he will probably find no difficulty in placing worthily on his walls.

TO LADIES AND AMATEURS.

"I too have my vocation,—work to do."

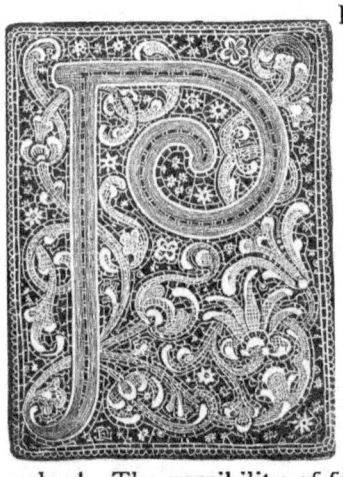

ERHAPS in no branch of industry is there greater waste of labour than in "ladies' work." How many women there are who have perpetually in hand some piece of fancy needle-work, and how few of them succeed in accomplishing anything that can justly lay claim to artistic value! The possibility of failure in art is, perhaps, avoided by abstaining from any attempt of the kind. Or the search after prettiness stands for an ideal. Often there is no higher aim than the having "something to do." The idea that art is within the scope or province of ladies in general has not entered into the heads of some of them, and they would be astonished to hear that, almost without exception, every one could, if she would, produce work which, humble as it might be, was really art. Yet that is no more than the truth. The scope of art is practically boundless ; it does not begin and end with the painting of pictures and the modelling of statues ; where there is room for workmanship there is room for it. This has been held to be so in all ages when art flourished, and perhaps the present revolt against the undue prestige attaching to picture painting, and the favour in which decorative art begins to be held, are signs that the modern revival is a reality and not merely a fashion.

The greatest art has always been of a decorative character ; but let it suffice for the present to assert that decorative art is, as such, second to no other ; that granted, we may admit that under the head of "decorative" are included also the lesser arts applied to industry. These arts have suffered from the slight esteem in which they have been held among us. "High art," so called, has been so far prejudicial to them that it has attracted, by its pretensions, the best of those whom nature had meant for decorators ; and many a one who might perhaps in the natural direction of his own genius have risen to fame, has dissipated his talent in vain attempts to paint pictures. If high art were less high the art of every-day would be higher.

A most dangerous will-o'-the-wisp is high art to amateurs, and to lady amateurs in particular. It must be remembered that the signal success of certain lady artists is the result of a devotion to art, and a sacrifice to it, that amateurs are scarcely prepared to offer. How many even of those ladies who really love art would be willing to shut themselves out from household pleasures and from household cares, and devote some six or eight hours daily to the study of it? how many of them, even though they might be willing, would feel themselves justified in doing so? Those who clamour for women's rights are not yet in a majority; ladies are for the most part content with their privileges, none the less precious for the duties with which they are associated. Assuming that lady amateurs do not, as a class, think of materially altering their mode of life, but simply desire to occupy their leisure pleasurably, and at the same time not unprofitably, in the pursuit of art, it would be better for them, and for art too, that they should realise at the outset that, though they may easily paint such pictures as give satisfaction to their friends, it is improbable that the paintings of many of them will have any great value as art. The conditions of their life are against it. On the other hand, society is so constituted that there is every encouragement for the less ambitious arts in which they have hitherto distinguished themselves, and for some in which they have not as yet made very great progress.

The most obvious opportunity for the exercise of a woman's artistic faculty seems to lie in needle-

work. She may not compete favourably with professional men in the picture galleries, but in such
delicate work as embroidery she has the game in
her own hands. The needle was her sceptre from
the first, and she has achieved with it royal results.
Yet her sphere does not end there. Wherever
there is question of taste, what might not woman's
influence do for art ? And how little it has actually
accomplished !

It has been said that one can detect at once on
entering a room what part a woman's hand has
had in its arrangement. That is true enough ; but
it is not an unqualified compliment to feminine tact
and taste. If the woman's influence is betrayed by
a sense of delicacy seldom found in men, and by a
neatness and propriety almost as rare among them,
it is still rather womanliness than any particular personality that is apparent ; and in place of anything
like character or individuality we find a gloss of
feeble fashionableness, or the evidence of an abiding
faith in the efficiency of upholstery and trimmings.
My lady's decoration is apt to be too suggestive
of the dressmaker or milliner. She is more likely
to think of a muslin blind to screen a window than
of delicately painted panes of glass. It is a very
natural error on her part that, in the practical
difficulties of an art she has not learned, she should
turn for help to the resources of a craft in which she
is more at home. None the less it is an error, and
the first step towards the exercise of a right influence

in domestic decoration is to recognise that it is an
art, that every art demands independent study, and
that the expedients of one art cannot be made to
supply the place of the natural resources of another.
All proficiency is power; one art is always willing
to come to the assistance of another ; a knowledge

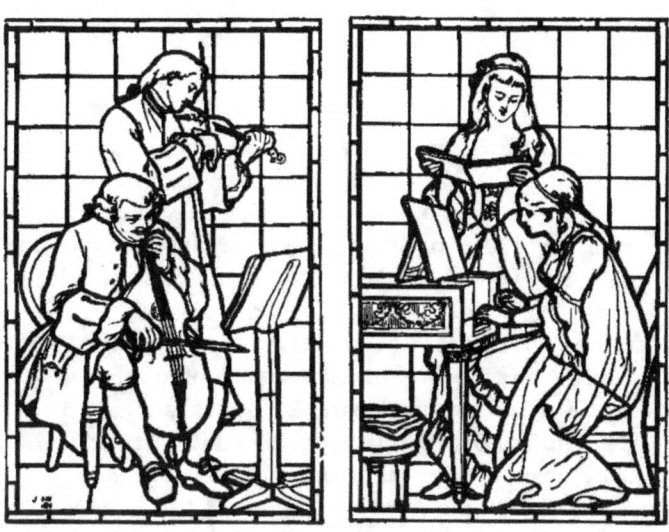

Painted window-panes.

of dressmaking, for example, may at times be of use
to the furnisher ; but it is only a skilful furnisher
who can turn it to that use ; and the attempt to
decorate a room from the dressmaker's point of
view, is certain to end in flimsiness and inconsistency.
We can seldom afford to dispense altogether with

drapery in a room, and no one will deny the grace and dignity of simple hangings, or the beauty of rich stuffs ; but where the furniture is all more or less *dressed up*, simplicity is out of the question. Pina-fores do not add to the elegance of a room, any more than they minister to our comfort, and it must be confessed that the toilet-table "got up" in muslin and pink satin, as if for a dance in the servants' hall, is not a triumph of art.

We hear constant reference to "the niceties of adornment which come with the presence of women" in the house. How far do these niceties compensate for the fuss, flimsiness, and fashion they introduced with them ? A bachelor's room may lack the charm that a woman's hand only can bestow. Yet bachelors do not sigh for the bright poker, and the clean hearth that looks so hard and inhospitable. They are reconciled to the absence of unnecessary curtains and antimacassars. They realise that order does not consist in putting things out of sight, and they have a horror of the demon of tidiness who hovers about the dwellings of so many men they know.

There is here no thought of depreciating in any way the feminine capacity. More often than not a man's wife is his "better half" indeed, without suggestion of irony in the title. If man be the superior animal, it is mainly as animal that he is superior. Whether superior or inferior to him, woman is certainly different from man ; her highest qualities are those in which man cannot compete

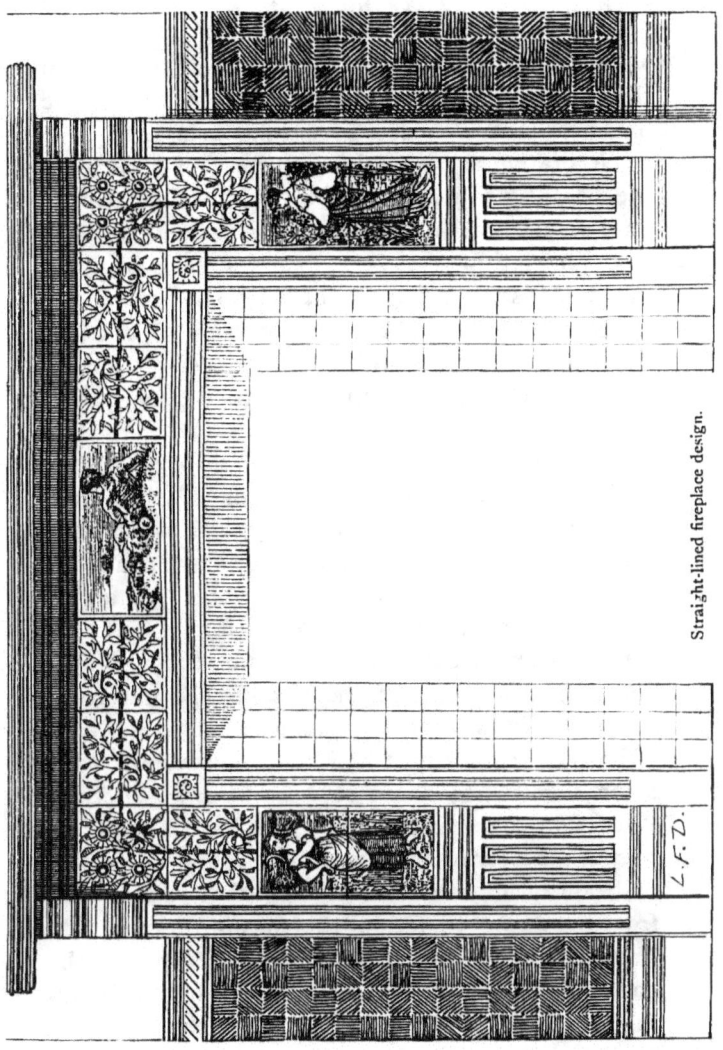

Straight-lined fireplace design.

with her, just as she cannot cope with him in things wherein his strength lies. With all the nattiness and delicacy which she brings to bear on decorative art, we miss largeness of treatment, breadth, originality, and self-restraint. The straight line, so needful in decoration, is hateful to her. The judicial faculty, on which (unrecognised) so much of taste depends, is not her *forte*.

Women have so much more occasion to consider questions of taste, that one might well expect of them something more than of the sterner half of the race. Men, dandies excepted, do not seriously debate the question of what shall be the pattern of their next waistcoat or the colour of their new trousers; they accept, half lazily, half scornfully, the goods that Snip provides; but women, all but a few of the stronger minded, devote time, at all events, to the consideration of costume, and with some of them it is the one engrossing topic of conversation. They ought, therefore, in the nature of things, to know something about taste, at least in reference to costume. And they would have something to say about it worth hearing, if their discussion concerning it had been based upon the idea of discovering what was most useful, becoming, or beautiful in dress; but, seeing that it starts all from the desire to follow the fashion, it not only does not tend to educate their taste, but, on the contrary, vitiates it. When we begin by confounding the folly of the hour with beauty that is of all time, the ultimate tangle of our ideas on taste is hopeless. Decorative art, more than all other, should be simple, unobtrusive, and modest. Fashion flaunts herself. Modesty and the modiste were never on the best of terms together. Our choice lies between art and fashion—either at the expense of the other.

What can women do towards the decoration of the home? In the first place they might leave undone something they are wont to do. They might begin by abstaining from the introduction of all unnecessary drapery and flimsiness. In manufacturing and other large towns, cleanliness and health alike recommend that as little stuff as possible be introduced into a room—reason the more for women to take care that what is admitted be of the best; they should be judges of textile fabrics.

It is probably still with the needle that most women would prefer to work towards the decoration of their rooms, and there is no reason why they should not do so; but the aim should be to make as beautiful as possible the necessary hangings in the room, not to introduce more stuffs simply for the sake of the needlework.

There is unlimited scope for the exercise of womanly tact and taste in the arrangement and furnishing of every room. The lady of the house might be within doors what the architect assumes to be—director and controller of everything, selecting all furniture and fittings with a view to

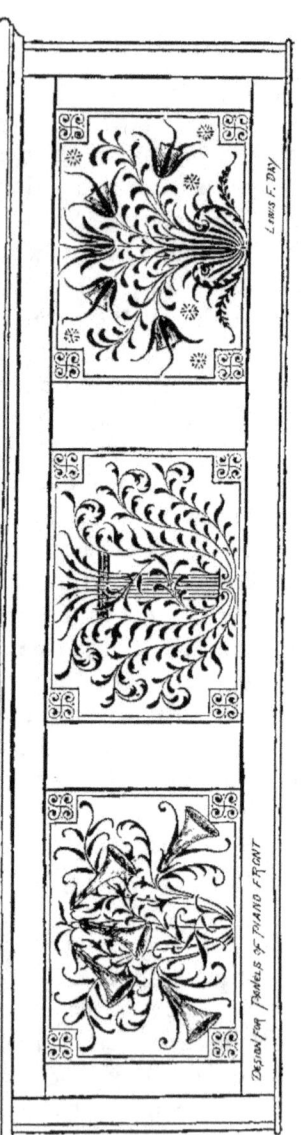

LEWIS F. DAY

DESIGN FOR PANELS OF PIANO FRONT

effect as well as fitness, combining all colours harmoniously, and seeing that all is executed with nicety and refinement. The fitting and furnishing of a room is to a very great extent a matter of detail, into which a busy man has seldom time to enter; and ladies, whose domain is the home, have every opportunity and many qualifications for the introduction of art into it. If only they could turn a deaf ear to the puffery of the latest novelty, and permit themselves to like or dislike without reference to what Mrs. Somebody may think, they could not fail to lead the art of every-day mainly in the direction in which it should go. They

would still have to beware of the seductions of
mere prettiness, which has such attractions for them.
The prettiness of a boudoir is all very well in a
boudoir, but it palls upon us when it pervades the
house. What we need in house-decoration is, first
of all fitness, and then beauty. But beauty is composed of many elements—strength, dignity, meaning, character, as well as grace of form and harmony
of colour. Prettiness is something considerably
less than beauty.

Those who desire really to control the taste dis-
played in their homes could not, perhaps, make a
better start than by proceeding to master the characteristics of ancient styles of ornament. " Style " is
a much abused word. In the mouth of one man it
means showiness; in another's it stands for the latest
craze—" Early English," " Queen Anne," or whatever it may be labelled ; whilst with others, more
learned but scarcely wiser, it is an excuse for the
substitution of pedantry in the place of art, and the
suppression of all originality. Every one has a
right to resent the attempt to impose a style upon
him. Our style must be the offspring of our own
individuality, and of the circumstances of our time
and country. But we cannot afford in these days
to be ignorant of the styles which have become
historic, and if we go contrary to them it should be,
not for want of knowing, but deliberately, with intent to be ourselves. It might be possible to a man
of judgment, even though he were not one of the

initiated, to bring together a medley of objects of all periods, which should yet form a harmonious whole. The safe plan, however, is to have some tolerably clear notion in our minds of the characteristics of the various styles that have been. And this does not come by intuition. It would be idle to expect that others than antiquaries or professional ornamentists should dive very deeply into the mysteries of style in ornament ; but some study of the subject is strongly to be recommended to anyone who wishes to run alone and yet not stray from the path of consistency. The published works on the subject are, without exception, too technical to recommend themselves ; but Mr. Wornum's able 'Analysis of Ornament' has the remarkable merit of brevity ; and one can scarcely rise from reading it without having gathered information on the subject.

The part that a lady can take in the execution of decorative work depends of course upon her artistic qualifications. There appears to be a notion prevalent that china-painting, panel-painting, and the like, are lesser arts that can be acquired in a few lessons, without previous training in art. Certainly a flat ornament is more easy to paint than a picture ; but then the flat ornament has to be designed, and the art of design is not learnt in a day. There would be no difficulty in finding ladies well able to paint oak leaves ; but most of them would find considerable difficulty in adapting them to decorative design. The truth, so obvious that one is half ashamed to have to reiterate it, is that only those who are prepared to work steadily and earnestly at the art they adopt, however small that

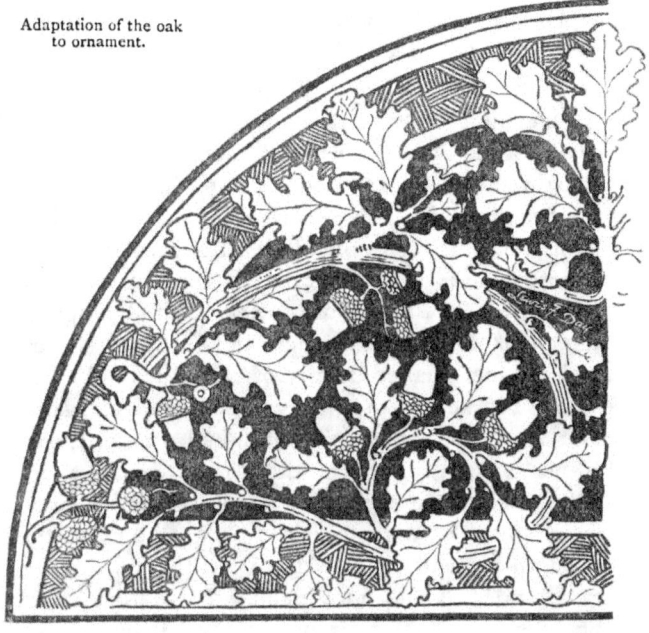

Adaptation of the oak to ornament.

art may be, are likely to produce anything in the least worth doing. The amateur needs to be advised that decoration is a much more serious matter than she imagines. She sees that a certain piece of trade-work lacks the delicacy or finish that would certainly have characterised it if she had done it ; but she does not in the least realise the amount of practice and experience which went to the doing of that piece of trade-work, without which practice and experience her superior refinement can find no adequate utterance. Her thoughts and sentiments, however admirable, need to be expressed grammatically, and unfortunately the grammar of art is not taught at school.

One difficulty that ladies have to contend with in decoration is that what is most available, and most wanted, is bold work, large in design and treatment, whilst ladies lean rather towards refinement and finish than breadth. It is work, too, that is best done *in situ*, and a lady is not quite at home on the top of the scaffold. She has fuller opportunity for the exercise of her talent on panels, tiles, and all the smaller details of furniture, and these details can be executed conveniently and at leisure. The cabinet or sideboard is useful all the same, and is not unsightly, whilst the panels are yet unpainted ; but the decoration of the walls of a room, which must be done quickly, is a tax upon the strength and endurance of the artist that few women can stand. A lady may paint a frieze for a room, but it will be better for her to paint it on canvas, being sure, however, to have it put up into its place from time to time, to see that she is not wasting labour, or worse. It is difficult even for experienced decorators to design at the easel work fit for its place at a distance. The less ambitious amateur,

if such there be, might do something to add interest
to the familiar wall-papers, upon which we have
so often to rely for effective decoration. In a
printed frieze of foliage, for example, the monotony of the inevitable repetition might be broken by
the introduction, at judicious intervals, of birds, or
butterflies, or other objects of interest. Even the
colour of the ordinary wall-paper might be vastly improved by touching the flowers and leaves, here and

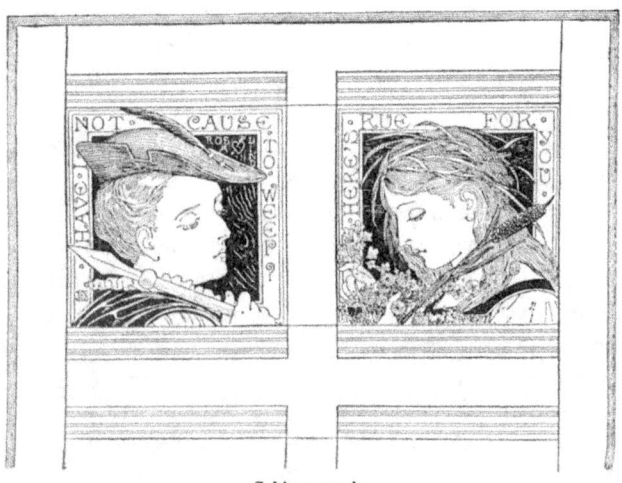

Cabinet panels.

there, by hand. The manufacturer is of course
limited to a small number of colour-blocks, but
there is no restriction, except that imposed by taste,
to the variety possible to him who works with his
hands. Similarly, embossed and gilded leather and

leather-paper will repay the labour of glazing them with transparent colour.   Gorgeous effects may be obtained by this simple process, which demands little more than an eye for colour.   Ambition is not greatly to be encouraged in amateurs.   It may safely be left to grow of itself with growing power.   It is a pity that unprofessional effort is mainly directed towards the production of objects which only rare artistic excellence can make worth having.   It is to be remembered that we judge more *useful* work with much greater leniency than that which has no other justification than beauty.

Perhaps the discretion which should suggest to the amateur to take up that class of work which the professional artist has neglected, would avail more than the valour which would rush into direct competition with him.   In all respects the work of ladies would be more available in domestic decoration, if it were less lofty in its aim.   The amateur burns always to do something of importance—figures probably, or at the very least flower-groups. But even if this ambition be warranted by ability, the occasion for a great deal of such prominent work seldom occurs in an ordinary living-room. There is, on the other hand, considerable scope for ornament of that more modest kind which is content to take its lowly place in the general effect.   This, however, is just the kind of work which has least attraction for the amateur, who is, for the most

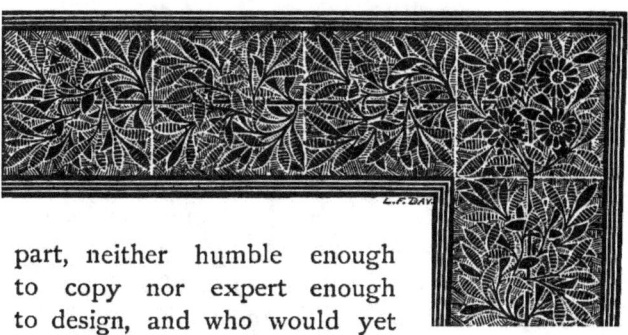

Unpretending tile painting.

part, neither humble enough to copy nor expert enough to design, and who would yet perhaps have some difficulty in drawing the simple curves of a scroll. Neither does such work earn the loud praise of those who measure success by the pretentiousness of the effort.

Men seem to think that women have no wish to hear the truth, and only hunger for applause and flattery. If that be so, there are plenty ready to supply their craving. Let here and there a solitary Goth be allowed to say frankly what he believes to be true. In so doing he does more honour to women than those who hold them in such slight esteem as to think that they can appreciate only what is pleasant. It was a woman who wrote beseeching men that they would " honour us with truth, if not with praise."

The simple truth, as it seems to me, is that ladies seldom give sufficient thought and study to decoration. If they have aptitude, they are too readily persuaded that they know all about it, when in reality their knowledge is rudimentary ; they are too impatient, too ambitious, too little aware of the difficulties before them, and of the limits of their ability. On the other hand, if they be modest they are wanting in self-reliance, they do not believe enough in themselves, and they allow their feeling to be overruled by those who, knowing less, talk more confidently. Needlework excepted, there is very little ladies' work done that is of real value in decoration, yet there is scarcely a young house-wife but might learn to do good work, worth doing in the house, but which, failing her, remains undone.

Let ladies talk less about "art-work," and culti-vate themselves more fully in art. If they have anything of the artist in them their work will be art-work, no matter whether it be executed with the needle or the brush. In one respect art is like murder—it *will out !*

It is the fault of the education of ladies that they realise so little what goes to make proficiency in decorative art or in anything. Their time has been spent in acquiring accomplishments which accomplish nothing. Their efforts are looked upon with the kindly leniency of friends, who would always rather not say anything that might give them pain, and are never put to the test which all bread-winning art must stand every time it comes to market. The lamentable outcome of this unkind kindness is that when a lady, as so often happens,

is reduced to want employment, she fancies that
the half-developed faculties which have been wont
to win the praise of friends, will enable her to
earn a livelihood.   It is sickening to think of the
gradual disillusion of such a poor gentlewoman, as
the truth of her position dawns upon her, and she
feels more and more how poorly she is equipped
for the struggle of life.   It is one of the pressing
questions of our time, How shall poor gentlewomen
support themselves?   Many imagine that the
career of art, and of decorative art especially, is
open to them.   So it is, or would be if they had
been trained to it. But ladies must not be offended
at being told the truth, so true that it is a truism,
that every trade, and every art, needs to be learnt.
The real source of their distress and trouble is in
the prejudice, which fathers hug to themselves with
more than feminine infatuation, that a man is degraded by allowing his daughters to work for their
living.   It is a sort of cowardice which allows a
man to hinder his daughter from perfecting herself
in anything that would enable her to stand alone,
and yet to leave her at his death at the mercy of
the world, with half-idle if not luxurious habits, a
showy but unavailable education, and prejudices
which it is too late to eradicate.   When a young
woman is all at once thrown upon her own
resources, with a necessity of earning immediately
her own living, those resources seldom prove
adequate, and that necessity of at once earning an

income makes impossible the study that should by rights have preceded the exercise of a craft, whatever it may be. A man should look things in the face, and if he is not in the position to leave his daughters so certainly provided for that their comfort is secured, it is his obvious duty to pocket his prejudice, and fit his children for the future that is before them. The only room for doubt is whether it is not the duty of every man, however rich, to bring up his children to know some one thing thoroughly. The accomplishments of a lady, and the education of a gentleman, are the most charming accompaniments of more useful knowledge, but they are no more than accompaniments, and are far from supplying its place. Once we have arrived at a certain proficiency in technique, these accomplishments begin to be valuable, but till then they are sometimes even a hindrance.

A lady who had seriously set herself in the days of prosperity to cultivate the taste which her education had left undeveloped, and to embellish her rooms with some idea beyond fashion or prettiness, might, in more straitened circumstances, find the experience of use to her. But it must be said that, as a rule, even the skilful amateur is anything but a useful assistant to the practical decorator, and the ladies who apply for "art-work," as it is called according to the cant current, apply too late; they are too old, and probably too well satisfied with their capacities, too anxious to earn something, too ignorant of the slight commercial value of such labour as they have to sell.

These are hard words to those who seek employment, but soft words that lead to disappointment are in reality more cruel. How poor gentlewomen may best support themselves is a serious question, not lightly to be solved. Few of them will be able to do so by means of decoration, or any other art or trade, to which they have not served some sort of apprenticeship. But there are many branches of decoration by any one of which they might live in comfort, if they had seriously studied it whilst yet there was no need of making profit of it. The advice that needs more than all other to be pressed upon those who may have to earn a livelihood by any art, is that they should learn it betimes, and before the need for self-support occurs. No doubt that need will act as a spur; but those who feel till then no inclination to serious study, will probably not be far wrong in concluding that they lack, not only the energy, but the ability which would insure success, even in the least of the every-day arts.

THE ORNAMENT OF THE FUTURE.

"In the coming by-and-by."

S it possible to discuss the orna-
ment of the future without enter-
ing upon prophecy ? It is not
much that we can foretell, but we
know that we are ourselves, day
by day, sowing the seeds of it.

The very slightest comparison
of ancient with modern ornament
will show that the conditions under which they
exist are altogether different. The earliest ornament is always either instinctive, or traditional, or
symbolic in its character ; perhaps in all of it
instinct, tradition, and symbolism are to be found.
The first impulse of the savage may have been to
beautify a paddle or an axe, and the idea of introducing a meaning into his work may have occurred
to him later. It is more likely that his first
thought was to represent something, and that it
was chiefly owing to his want of skill, his limited
appliances, and his clear perception that use was
of much higher importance than imagery, that
led to such a representation of nature as we are
accustomed to call conventional. The continual

reproduction of the same symbols would in itself lead naturally to a less realistic and less intelligible rendering of them; just as our signatures, which we write so often that we write them mechanically, have a way of developing (or degenerating) into something that is little more than a hieroglyphic. In the same way the names of railway stations become, from constant repetition, undistinguishable on the lips of porters; and the cries of itinerant vendors in the streets are intelligible only through our familiarity with the sounds.

It is improbable that there should be no symbolism whatever underlying the spirals, lines, and bands of savage art; and, on the other hand, even the obviously symbolic ornament of the Egyptians shows considerable feeling for the purely sensuous side of art. In every development of ancient art, tradition, sense, and symbolism have all been at work, the one or the other predominant, according to the temperament and stage of civilisation of the nation that produced it.

Modern art exists under quite other conditions. No one seems to want symbolism; it is scarcely tolerated among us; and instinctive art is as much a thing of the past as ballad poetry. As to tradition, only when we have determined which of the principles underlying ancient art have lived out their lives, and which of them are really alive, can we turn it to account. Of the living principles it concerns us further to know which will bear transplanting, and are likely to thrive in the atmosphere of the nineteenth century. The conditions under which the art of every-day is produced have changed by degrees so imperceptible that it seems scarcely to have been aware of the movement, and has not kept pace with it. It is only recently that we have awoke to the degraded condition into which ornament had lapsed, and realise the urgent need of improvement, if our manufactures are to hold their own in the world.

There were times when ornament was produced without a thought of the traffic in it. Now it is the traffic that gives rise to ornament. We cannot, therefore, leave commerce out of account, since trade is no longer simply the outlet for the arts applied, but in a great measure the origin of them. It is a pity that there should ever be antagonism between artist and manufacturer. Each is only too ready to make use of the other, and to form an alliance with that personal end in view. But while each party to the bargain looks only to his own interest, the cause of neither is likely to prosper. Since they are dependent one upon the other, since for good or ill their fate is knit together, and divorce between them is impossible, they had best come to a clear understanding, and work together for the common good.

The conditions of other days may have been more favourable to art than the present state of things. We who live in the present and know so

well where it pinches, are inclined to look back long-
ingly to a past of whose hardships we have had no
experience. But it is with the present that we
have to do. Nor can we long maintain an attitude
of opposition to its spirit. Strong men may to
some extent direct the age they live in ; but to
resist it is idle, and to wail is foolish. Whether
we like it or no, machinery and steam-power,
and electricity for all we know, will have something to say concerning the ornament of the
future.

No artist will think of denying that the highest
art is of necessity hand-work. No machine can
approach the best work of men's hands. And even
in the arts of every-day there must always be
room for actual handicraftsmen. But they will inevitably be in that minority in which the most
accomplished find themselves always. The popular
demand is for machine work. Its smoother and
cleaner finish, its cheapness, and the certainty with
which it can be produced, more than outweigh
in public opinion the artistic merits of rougher,
costlier, and less certain results. The practical
and commercial mind of those in whose hands the
matter mainly rests, is not likely to be swayed by
our sentimental regrets ; and the discussion of the
relative merits of art and manufacture is, therefore,
to little purpose. It has practically been settled
by the public that they want machine-work, and
they mean to have it. We may protest that they

have chosen unwisely, but they will not pay much heed to us. We may shrug our shoulders and retire, if we can afford that luxury, to the select and solitary enjoyment of our own ideas ; but in so doing we leave our art at the mercy of those who neither know nor care about it, and the last state of ugliness to which they deliver it up will be worse than the first. It is a question whether the perfect precision now possible by means of modern mechanical contrivances might not, rightly applied, be as valuable in ornament as it is actually pernicious.

We cannot do without common-sense, even though at times it be so common as not greatly to commend itself to us. Men who live by their art have as little right to despise the pecuniary considerations attaching to its connection with manufacture and commerce as to pander to what they believe to be vulgarity, or prostitute their art to money-getting. The profit that an artist derives from commerce puts him in a better position to carry out his own idea of what is best in art, and to insist upon a higher and still higher standard of excellence in the manufacture for which he designs. There is scarcely a branch of manufacture that is beneath the consideration of the designer, provided only he be allowed to do his best. The work that degrades is that in which he is forced to work under his strength, placing himself upon the level of an ignorant or stupid employer. The producer who has some knowledge of art and believes thoroughly in its commercial value, is its best patron. The worst is the Mr. Brooke of commerce, who has faith in its efficacy only " up to a certain point." His instructions to the artist are always, " Something saleable, now ! " He doctors the designs he has purchased, purges them of all that had any value as art in them, and then, when the enfeebled result of his experiment appeals to no one, he complains that " Art may be all very well in its way, you know, but the public do not appreciate it; they want something attractive, something showy now ! " He has a long list of epithets at the tip of his tongue, all of which, being interpreted, mean " vulgar."

" Thirty millions, mostly fools," was the cry of the Jeremiah of our own time. The manufacturer appears to think that the millions are mostly vulgar. He may be right or wrong ; but it is to be hoped that there is a public also for the taste that is not loud. The fit audience is alway few. For all that, the highest wisdom may not consist in lowering our standard to the imagined level of the many. The fact that the public accepts a poor bait, is no proof that it would not more greedily seize a richer one.

There is no compromise possible with vulgarity. Those who like it prefer it undiluted, and those who have taste are disgusted by the least taint of it. You cannot well catch two publics with one bait, but you may easily miss them both.

The manufacturer, as such, does not pretend to care for art, as such, and we have no right to expect from him much sympathy for it ; but it is only reasonable to insist that every man should be allowed to do his best. Those who have sufficient faith in art to invite the co-operation of the artist, might well have confidence enough in their own choice to produce the work designed by him in its entirety, and as he designed it. Were artists truer to themselves in this respect, less afraid of losing a patron, more certain that the most fatal mistake of all in art is to do less than our utmost, then the education of the public and the ultimate improvement of every-day art would be only a question of time.

We are apt to forget that art is only what its name implies, a means to an end, or, more strictly speaking, a means of utterance, an expression of ourselves. It is of infinitely more importance what we are, and what we have to say, than how we say it. But the force of an argument depends very much upon the facility with which it is expressed, and, among cultivated people, there is naturally a strong prejudice in favour of speech that is grammatical.

It is the gift, not only of the poet, but of every artist, to see and to say. In the greatest artists the two faculties are so well matched that it is impossible to dissociate the thought from its expression ; in others, less gifted, it is often only too painfully evident that a fine thought is strangled in the bringing forth, or that the flowing expression clothes a lean imagination. Of the twin powers of seeing and saying, the first takes natural precedence. But the world has little tolerance for the seer who cannot fitly deliver his message. On the other hand, men are only too tolerant of that most intolerable of men who can express himself fluently but has nothing worth saying to say. It has arrived at this :—we admit the supremacy of the twofold gift, but next to that we place the mere power of expression. There is just this excuse for the preference of the lesser power, that it is available ; and people who pride themselves upon being practical prefer a quality that can be turned to account.

For all useful purposes, the discussion of art must be, to a very great extent, technical. We must let every man choose his own theme, and limit our criticism to the manner in which he works it out—that is to say, his art. When we wish to discuss the subject of his discourse, we pass beyond the artist to the man ; and when we propose to direct him in this respect, it is the man, rather than the artist, that we have to deal with.

Futile as it may be to criticise the artist instead of his art, the attempt to realise the relation of a man to his work, and the influence of character upon art, need not be equally unprofitable. National temperament is very plainly marked in national art.

The savage or the cultivated, the sluggish or the
volatile, the energetic or the sensuous, the restrained
or the extravagant nations, may be recognised in
their art.   Frenchmen seldom paint goody-goody
pictures, and Englishmen do not delight in the
portrayal of ghastly horrors.   Gallic lightness of
touch and insular restraint are more than merely
artistic qualities.   It is possible, however, that in
the future, art may arrive at a more cosmopolitan
character.   We may be certain that it will march
with the times.   One can form no fair opinion of the
present condition of art, and of its hope in the near
future, without taking into account the influence
of the social atmosphere upon us as men.   As we
are, so our art will be, even our decorative art ; and
we are what we are, partly by birth, but very much
by surrounding influence.   For all the want of
"style" in our ornament it is brim-full of the characteristics of the nineteenth century.   Only in an age
of railways and screw steamers, an age of cheap
reproduction and photography, an age of colossal
fortunes and organised labour, could such art be
possible.   The incongruity of modern design is the
inevitable consequence of the sudden accumulation of examples of more kinds of art than we
can digest at once—some that are, perhaps,
absolutely indigestible—resulting in a surfeit of
good things, from which no former age was in a
position to suffer.   Our ornament is of its century,
inasmuch as it is prosaic and mechanical, fickle,

"fast," self-assertive, and none too lofty in its ambition ; nor is it guiltless of the besetting sin of the age we live in—cleverness.   On the brighter side our art shows something of the deeper and more general knowledge that is within the scope of this generation.   Facilities of travel have done something to lighten our native darkness as to what is decorative ; illustrated books on the subject have had a similar influence upon us ; and our art is the better for it.   Modern commercial enterprise, if it has not encouraged the best, has certainly stimulated the production of design, and it is in some measure owing to it that at the present day the art of ornament is at least alive.

The proof of its vitality is that it grows or tries its hardest to grow.   Antiquaries would fain insist that it has no business to grow.   They are not quite agreed among themselves as to the precise date at which art expired, but they concur in the theory that art is dead, and all that they would leave to us is a sort of mummy, which we should do well to regard reverently, since it is all that remains of the beauty that once was.   Happily, the modern spirit of eclecticism which is their abhorrence, (perhaps because in it they feel instinctively the natural enemy of all their race,) is evidence of the life remaining in modern art.

Few artists, if any, have been without reverence for the art of their foregoers ; none certainly ever showed his reverence by gaping at it in sterile

admiration ; on the contrary it stimulated him to
do something, not like it, but which, except for
it, he never would have done.   And so in all
times, where there has been art there has been
growth.   Go back to old work for inspiration and
guidance, by all means.   The first lesson we learn
from it is altogether in harmony with common-
sense, and contrary to the teaching of Dry-as-dust.
It is the work of artists, not of archæologists ; and
whatever style they adopted, that they adapted
to their own ways and wants.   In all ancient
work style was more or less traditional.   Certain
forms and certain symbols were handed down from
generation to generation, modified, perhaps, in
transit, but subject to no sudden change.   One
style grew out of another gradually ; deliberate
innovation would not have been tolerated ; and
a general ignorance of what was going on in other
parts of the world, kept men out of the way of
temptation to go astray.   Under Eastern despotism the types of ornament were fixed and almost
unalterable.   In the West, art developed more
rapidly under more enlightened rule.   If Gothic
art, as it progressed, absorbed the ideas of the times,
it was unaffected by what was going on in China
or Japan.

In the art of the future, outgrowth of ancient
art though it be, there must be more of free choice.
Already the times are out of joint with despotism ;
we no longer act according to tradition ; we are not

unsophisticated as savages, in bondage like the Egyptians, isolated like the Chinese, cultivated like the Greeks, bigoted like the Arabs or the early Christians. We cannot go back. If we do not know enough to do better work than our ancestors, we know too much to be content with any of it. Each new field of study that is opened to us tempts us afresh. We are unsettled. We cannot quite make up our minds whether we will found our style on Greek or Gothic, Renaissance or Roman, Japanese or Jacobean, or even on " Queen Anne." Our eyes are opened to the idea of style, and we are haunted by the consciousness of it. We have gathered a heap of ornamental treasure round us, till it hems in our movements, and imprisons our ideas.

Badly as we may be in want of a style of the nineteenth century, we cannot consent to put up with the galvanised mummy of any dead art. We torment ourselves over-much about style. If we only keep our eyes open and our wits at work, and do honestly our best, we need not fear that our work will be altogether contemptible in the eyes of a civilisation to come. Perhaps when art is more cosmopolitan the individuality of the workman may be more esteemed. A man betrays himself in his work. If his aim be merely money or notoriety, he may accomplish his end ; but, failing to accomplish himself as an artist, his art will scarcely live. If a capable man have to do mere journey-work for

bare subsistence, that too will be seen, and there
will be a pathetic interest in that. Whether we be
serious or in jest, plodding or impatient, self-centred
or impressionable, the work of our hands will show
our sympathies and our antipathies ; even our crot-
chets will crop up in our designs. No thoughtful
artist can fail to see how the accidents of his education have influenced his art. He knows that he
would never have done just what he does, if he had
not been abroad, if at some critical period in his study
he had not come under the influence of some master
or masterpiece, some author or book perhaps, if he
had been either more or less fortunate in his career.
Each of us can account to himself for the obvious
difference between his own work and another's,
and explain much of the individuality in the work
of his friends. If it were not for this individuality,
only the most consummate masterpieces of art
would be endurable, and some of us in our hearts
would like even them less, if we could catch no
glimpse of the man behind them.

In the art of every-day we cannot afford to spare
that element of interest. We may each of us do
this much towards the style of the future, that we
can in our work express ourselves, our own thought,
not another's, whatever may be preached to us to
the contrary. Our only care should be that the
thoughts and feelings we express be worthy. Our
art cannot be separate from what we are as men.
And this is certain ; if we are in earnest, if our

heart be in sympathy with the times, and if we put our heart into our work, the antiquary, and what is more, the artist of the future, will find in what we leave behind a something which will be equivalent to the style of the nineteenth century.

www.ingramcontent.com/pod-product-compliance
Lightning Source LLC
Chambersburg PA
CBHW071251220526
45468CB00001B/78